WORKING WITH METAL

TIME
LIFE ®
BOOKS

This volume is part of a series offering homeowners
detailed instructions on repairs, construction
and improvements they can undertake themselves.

HOME REPAIR
AND IMPROVEMENT

WORKING WITH METAL

BY THE EDITORS OF
TIME-LIFE BOOKS

TIME-LIFE BOOKS
ALEXANDRIA, VIRGINIA

Time-Life Books Inc.
is a wholly owned subsidiary of
TIME INCORPORATED

Founder	Henry R. Luce 1898-1967

Editor-in-Chief	Henry Anatole Grunwald
President	J. Richard Munro
Chairman of the Board	Ralph P. Davidson
Executive Vice President	Clifford J. Grum
Chairman, Executive Committee	James R. Shepley
Editorial Director	Ralph Graves
Group Vice President, Books	Joan D. Manley
Vice Chairman	Arthur Temple

TIME-LIFE BOOKS INC.

Managing Editor	Jerry Korn
Board of Editors	George Constable, George G. Daniels, Thomas H. Flaherty Jr., Martin Mann, Philip W. Payne, John Paul Porter, Gerry Schremp, Gerald Simons
Planning Director	Dale M. Brown
Art Director	Tom Suzuki
Assistant	Arnold C. Holeywell
Director of Administration	David L. Harrison
Director of Operations	Gennaro C. Esposito
Director of Research	Carolyn L. Sackett
Assistant	Phyllis K. Wise
Director of Photography	Robert G. Mason
Assistant	Dolores A. Littles
Chairman	John D. McSweeney
President	Carl G. Jaeger
Executive Vice Presidents	John Steven Maxwell, David J. Walsh
Vice Presidents	George Artandi, Stephen L. Bair, Peter G. Barnes, Nicholas Benton, John L. Canova, Beatrice T. Dobie, Carol Flaumenhaft, James L. Mercer, Herbert Sorkin, Paul R. Stewart

HOME REPAIR AND IMPROVEMENT

Editor	John Paul Porter

Editorial Staff for Working With Metal

Senior Editors	Robert M. Jones, Betsy Frankel
Designer	Edward Frank
Picture Editor	Adrian Allen
Text Editors	Lynn R. Addison, Brooke Stoddard (principals), Robert A. Doyle, Victoria W. Monks, Mark M. Steele, William Worsley
Writers	Tim Appenzeller, Patricia C. Bangs, Carol Corner, Rachel Cox, Kathleen M. Kiely, Kirk Y. Saunders, Mary-Sherman Willis
Researcher	Marilyn Murphy
Copy Coordinator	Diane Ullius Jarrett
Art Associates	George Bell, Fred Holz, Lorraine D. Rivard, Peter Simmons
Picture Coordinator	Betsy Donahue
Editorial Assistant	Cathy A. Sharpe
Special Contributor	Wendy Murphy (text)

EDITORIAL OPERATIONS

Production Director	Feliciano Madrid
Assistants	Peter A. Inchauteguiz, Karen A. Meyerson
Copy Processing	Gordon E. Buck
Quality Control Director	Robert L. Young
Assistant	James J. Cox
Associates	Daniel J. McSweeney, Michael G. Wight
Art Coordinator	Anne B. Landry
Copy Room Director	Susan B. Galloway
Assistants	Celia Beattie, Ricki Tarlow

Correspondents: Elisabeth Kraemer (Bonn); Margot Hapgood, Dorothy Bacon (London); Susan Jonas, Lucy T. Voulgaris (New York); Maria Vincenza Aloisi, Josephine du Brusle (Paris); Ann Natanson (Rome). Valuable assistance was also provided by: Caroline Alcock, Milly Trowbridge (London); John Dunne (Melbourne); Donna Lucey (New York); Ernie Shirley (Queensland); Mimi Murphy (Rome); Peter Allen (Sydney).

THE CONSULTANTS: Roswell W. Ard is a consulting structural engineer and a professional home inspector in northern Michigan. He has written professional papers on house construction.

Tom Bidwell is a self-taught blacksmith who has been in business in the Washington, D.C., area since 1973. He specializes in tool repairing and forging.

Bob Brookshire, owner of Brooktronics Engineering Sales and Technology in Laurel, Maryland, specializes in manufacturing electroplating equipment and in metalwork refurbishing.

Charles Hughes, chairman of the Washington, D.C., chapter of the American Welding Society, has been a welding instructor since 1963.

Colin Main is the sheet-metal shop foreman for a metal-fabricating company in Northern Virginia that specializes in plumbing, heating and air-conditioning installation.

Harris Mitchell, special consultant for Canada, has worked in the field of home repair and improvement since 1950. He is Homes editor of *Today* magazine and author of a syndicated newspaper column, "You Wanted to Know," as well as a number of books on home improvement.

Paul Ponzelli is the owner and operator of Suburban Welding Company, Alexandria, Virginia, specializing in security and ornamental ironworking. He is a member of the National Ornamental and Miscellaneous Metals Association.

For information about any Time-Life book, please write:
Reader Information
Time-Life Books
541 North Fairbanks Court
Chicago, Illinois 60611

Library of Congress Cataloguing in Publication Data
Time-Life Books.
    Working with metal.
    (Home repair and improvement; 30)
    Includes index.
    1. Metal-work. I. Time-Life Books.
    II. Series.
TT205.W64   684'.09   81-14339
ISBN 0-8094-3470-9   AACR2
ISBN 0-8094-3471-7 (lib. bdg.)
ISBN 0-8094-3472-5 (regular)
ISBN 0-8094-3473-3 (pbk.)

Contents

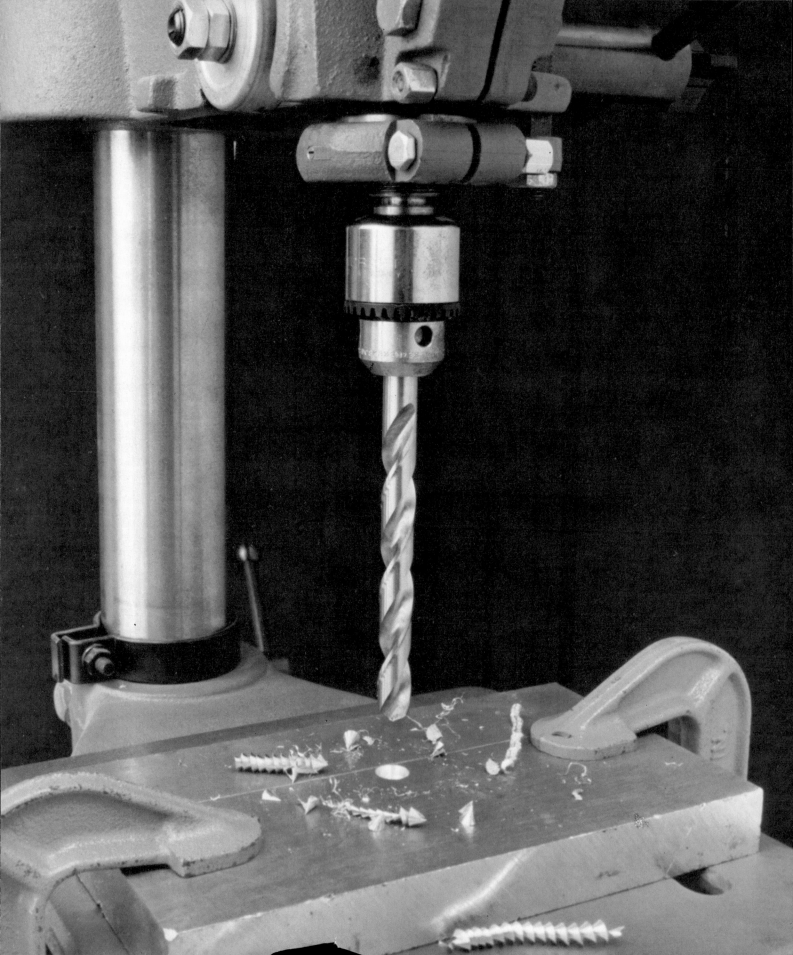

1 The Many Mutations of Metal

Remarkable precision. A drill press, fitted with a high-speed steel twist bit, makes short work of boring a hole through inch-thick aluminum plate. Securing the workpiece to the table of the drill press with C clamps makes it possible to align the bit precisely before drilling and to keep the metal from turning while the hole is bored—making it possible to achieve tolerances as close as four thousandths of an inch.

Whether as a porch rail, a hinge or a hoe blade, metal is prized for its hardness and strength. It can stand up to loads and conditions that would instantly shatter—or slowly rot away—most other materials. Yet for all its brawny virtues, metal is the most mutable of materials—both in its manufacture and after you get it home.

At the refinery, smeltery or mill, the very chemical composition of metal can be changed to suit its intended use. Iron, hardened with just a trace of carbon, becomes mild steel—a material malleable enough to be bent into rails or balustrades and ductile enough to be drawn thin for guying wire or piping. With more carbon, iron becomes tool steel—a product hard enough to cut, pierce or grind most other metals. Similar alchemies can be performed with other metals: Copper mixed with tin makes bronze, an alloy far easier to cast than pure copper; aluminum, used in its pure state for high-voltage electric lines, is transformed into far tougher duralumin with an admixture of manganese, copper and magnesium.

But matching metal to its intended use does not stop at the factory gate. At home you are just as free to alter the size and shape of metal, and in some cases its physical properties as well. The most dramatic changes, of course, are achieved when the metal is returned to its molten state with a torch or a furnace; the use of heating equipment for cutting, welding, forging and casting is explained in Chapter 3. A surprising number of manipulations, however, can be accomplished without heat. Specialized snips, cold chisels, saber saws fitted with ferrous blades, and hacksaws all make short work of cutting cold metal to size. High-speed twist bits pierce it easily, and an incredible array of manufactured fasteners—from tiny pop rivets to machine bolts as thick as a man's wrist—are available to join it. Metalworking tools called taps and dies are used to thread metal pieces themselves to serve as their own fasteners, and specialized jigs and bending tools—many of them homemade—facilitate altering its shape.

Yet for all the ease with which it can be rent, bent, pierced and polished, metal is ultimately a material that demands—and deserves—precision. For one thing, seldom can mistakes be fixed easily. Holes drilled in the wrong place cannot simply be puttied over and redrilled. A slightly wayward joint cannot easily be straightened out. But the precision required is a reward in itself; and the pleasure of a finely crafted balustrade or bracket will last long enough to justify the few extra hours necessary to craft it properly. Witness, for instance, the finely wrought iron grilles, many elaborately embellished with quatrefoils and fleurs-de-lis, that still guard the windows and doors of Venice. They were forged decades before Christopher Columbus set foot in the Americas.

The Basics: Alloys, Characteristics, Shapes

Metals for the home workshop come in a tremendous array of types, sizes and shapes. When you buy these metals they are, of course, cold and hard; but all of them have previously been heated to a liquid state and, while liquid, were purified of unwanted elements or mixed with certain new ones according to precise recipes. The products that result from these recipes number in the thousands: Metal makers offer not only pure metals but many alloys, each with unique ingredients and properties.

One metal and its family of alloys are so commonly used that they are set aside from the others and called ferrous, from the Latin *ferrum*, meaning "iron." This metal, whose ore constitutes about 5 per cent of the earth's crust, is used to make wrought iron, cast iron, and an alloy highly prized for its versatility, steel. The iron alloy with the lowest carbon content, actually a very low-carbon steel, is commonly—but incorrectly—known as wrought iron; true wrought iron, which is virtually pure iron, is difficult to find. Cast iron, on the other hand, contains more carbon than steel does, usually between 2 and 4 per cent. Cast iron is cast in molds to make heavy-duty articles such as machine bodies and engine blocks; it is both strong and brittle.

The principal alloy of iron is steel; in its simplest form this alloy is called plain, or carbon, steel and is divided into three categories depending on the carbon content. Low-carbon steel, also called mild steel, contains less than .3 per cent carbon. It is relatively easy to bend, drill and cut and is sold in a vast array of shapes, making it a favorite for cold-metal work. Medium-carbon steel, containing .3 to .6 per cent carbon, is harder and is the main component of many shop tools, such as hammers and clamps. High-carbon steel, the hardest, makes good cutting tools after it is given a special heat treatment that reduces its brittleness.

Besides having carbon added for hardness, steel can be altered by the addition of rarer metals. Adding chromium, for example, makes the steel stainless—that is, corrosion-resistant. Vanadium, a ductile metal, keeps steel from being brittle. Tungsten, which has a high melting point, produces steel that stays hard at high temperatures.

Whereas steels have long formed an extensive family of metals, aluminum has flourished since the 1940s as king of another wide-ranging empire of alloys. The addition of copper, zinc or manganese, for example, hardens and strengthens aluminum. These and other aluminum alloys have many advantages over steel. For one, they do not rust. They are also lighter in weight, they are available in as many shapes and sizes as steel, and they are easy to bend, drill, cut and cast.

Copper and its alloys, most notably brass and bronze, form a third group of easily worked metals. Copper can be bent, cut and hammered and is sold in sheets, bars, plates and wire. Bronze and brass, which do not corrode as rapidly as pure copper, make excellent household hinges, railings and locks.

Metals such as zinc, tin, silver and gold also find their way into home metalworking shops. Tin and zinc are most common as protective coatings, applied to slow the corrosion of iron and steel. Silver and gold are used on a smaller scale, mostly for making jewelry.

As different as their qualities are, many metals and alloys cannot be distinguished by their appearance. They are differentiated by numbering systems.

A precise system for identifying types of steel was developed by the Society of Automotive Engineers (SAE) and the American Iron and Steel Institute (AISI). In this system each steel alloy bears a four-digit number. The first digit indicates the type: 1 is carbon steel, 2 is nickel steel, 3 is nickel-chromium steel and so on. The second digit generally represents the percentage of the main alloying metal, and the last two digits give the approximate percentage of carbon content (these last two figures always represent tenths or hundredths of a per cent). For example, 1020 is a plain carbon steel containing about .2 per cent carbon—a mild steel; 4130 is a molybdenum steel with about 1 per cent of the second alloying metal, in this case chromium, and about .3 per cent carbon.

Aluminum alloys also have a four-digit numbering system. The first digit indicates the major alloying metal: 1 is almost pure aluminum, 2 is copper, 3 is manganese, and so on. The last three digits represent modifications to the alloy.

Such identification numbers will often be stamped on stock metal, but traditionally many suppliers have developed individual systems of their own, using colors as well as numbers. The best way to keep track of the different metals in your home shop is to devise your own code and to keep the metals organized.

Identification of unmarked metal starts as guesswork, but the guess can be refined by certain tests. One test is a check for magnetism. With a few exceptions, such as nickel and some stainless steels, the ferrous metals are magnetic, nonferrous ones nonmagnetic.

Another test is to press the metal on a grinding wheel and examine the sparks. Comparing these sparks to those produced by known pieces in your shop serves as a reasonable, if not certain, method of identification. In general, mild steel produces a long, straight, yellowish stream of sparks. As the carbon content of steel increases, the spark stream becomes shorter and fuller, and includes tiny explosions. Cast iron throws a small red spark, nickel a tiny orange spark, and other nonferrous metals, such as aluminum, no spark at all.

In a well-organized workshop, identifying metals will rarely be a problem. Metal stock should be stored on racks above the floor, segregated by metal type and shape. Hand tools are conveniently near if organized over the workbench on a heavy-duty pegboard. And a steel cabinet with a lock, fitted with pegboard above and shelves below, will protect such valuable equipment as taps, dies and measuring tools.

There are two types of workbenches, general-use and specialty. If you have room for only one, choose a variation of the standard woodworker's bench, and make it the regular height—about 34 inches. If you have room for a second, design it for specialized tasks such as welding or hammering; for comfort, make it several inches lower. Allow room on a bench for metalworking vises or bending devices of your choice; but if you want an anvil, plan to mount it on its own support.

Identification Aids by Appearance and Use

Metal or alloy	Surface	Interior	Properties	Uses
Cast iron	Dull gray	Silvery white or gray	Hard, brittle; rusts slowly	Engine blocks, machine bases, fireplace equipment, bathtubs
Steel				
Low-carbon (mild)	Dark gray or rusty; may have black scales	Bright silvery gray	Soft, bendable; easy to work; rusts quickly	Wrought-iron work; furniture, fencing, architectural trim
Medium-carbon	Dark gray or rusty; may have black scales	Bright silvery gray	Hard and strong; rusts quickly	Nuts, bolts, axles, pins
High-carbon (tool)	Dark gray or rusty; may have black scales	Bright silvery gray	Hard, brittle; rusts quickly	Cutting tools, hand tools
Stainless	Clean silvery gray	Bright grayish silver	Tough; difficult to work; does not rust or corrode	Kitchenware, furniture, picture frames, sinks
Aluminum	Gray to white, dull or bright	Silvery white	Light, soft, malleable; very easy to work or cast	Siding, roofing, gutters, flashing, auto and marine parts
Copper	Reddish brown to green	Bright copper	Soft; easy to work; good electricity conductor	Wiring and plumbing; major component of brass and bronze
Brass and bronze (copper combined with zinc or tin, and other metals)	Yellow, green or brown	Reddish yellow	Soft; can be worked hot or cold; casts and polishes well	Marine fittings, architectural trim, bearings
Nickel	Dark silvery gray, some green	Bright silvery white	Strong, hard; corrosion-resistant	Plating, alloys
Nickel-copper (Monel)	Dark gray	Light gray	Stronger and harder than nickel; corrosion-resistant	Corrosion-resistant construction
Lead	Bluish gray	White	Very heavy and soft; poisonous; corrosion-resistant	Protective linings, solder (with tin), alloys
Tin	Gray	Silvery white	Soft, malleable; corrosion-resistant	Galvanizing, alloys
Pewter (tin, antimony and copper)	Gray	White	Soft, casts well; modern pewter contains no lead, making it nonpoisonous	Eating utensils, decorative items
Zinc	Bluish gray	Bluish white	Soft but brittle; corrosion-resistant	Galvanizing, alloys
Silver	Dull gray	Bright silver	Soft; easy to work and cast	Eating utensils, decorative items, plating, solder
Gold	Yellow	Bright gold	Soft but tough; corrosion-resistant; easy to work and cast	Jewelry, electronics work, plating

Metal properties and uses. Listed vertically on the chart are metals a home metalworker is likely to encounter, whether in a pure state, as alloys or as protective coverings for other metals. In columns to the right each metal's surface color, interior color, prominent properties and major uses as listed, as aids in identification.

Shapes and Terminology

A shape for every need. Metal stock, especially steel and aluminum, is available in many standard shapes, ready to be cut, threaded, bent or joined. In the left column of this chart are cross sections of the most common stock shapes; the columns to the right give their names and indicate how they are sized. Some dealers will also take orders for shapes custom-extruded to virtually any specification.

Channels, I beams and H beams have two parallel arms, called flanges, connected by a perpendicular piece called the web. Although the conventions of metal measurement may be confusing to a layman in some instances, the metal industry adheres to the following terminology: The length of a flange from end to end is called flange width, and the length of the web is called the depth of the shape.

Shape	Name	Method of measurement
	Angle	Leg length by leg length by leg thickness
	Strip or band	Thickness by width (pieces ¼" and thicker are flats, pieces wider than 12" are sheets)
	Channel	Depth (web length) by web thickness by flange width
	Flat	Thickness by width (pieces 3/16" thick and less are strips or bands, pieces wider than 8" are plates)
	Hexagon, octagon	Width (from side to side, not corner to corner)
	Round tube or pipe	Outside diameter by wall thickness
	Square tube, rectangular tube	Outside width (by outside height for rectangular tube) by wall thickness
	I Beam, H Beam	Depth (web length) by web thickness by flange width
	Plate	Thickness by width (pieces 3/16" thick and less are sheets, pieces 8" wide and less are flats)
	Round or rod	Diameter
	Sheet	Thickness by width (pieces ¼" and thicker are plates, pieces 12" wide and less are strips or bands)
	Square	Width

Work Surfaces, Sturdy and Custom Designed

A metal-surfaced wooden bench. A metalworking bench built of wood should be very sturdy, with 4-by-4 or doubled 2-by-4 legs and a top made of solid wood at least 1½ inches thick. To protect the top, buy 12-gauge sheet steel *(page 38)* the same length as the bench top and two inches wider. Bend down a 1-inch flange along the front edge of the sheet, and bend up another along the back edge. Attach the steel sheet to the front edge and to the backboard with round-head wood screws driven through predrilled holes in the flanges.

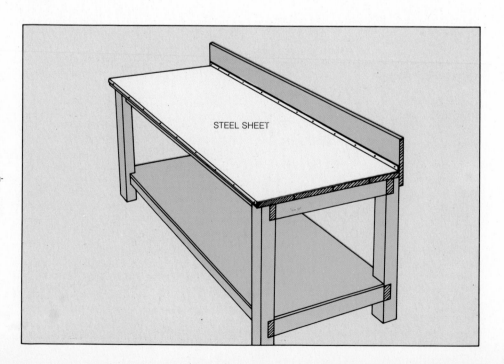

STEEL SHEET

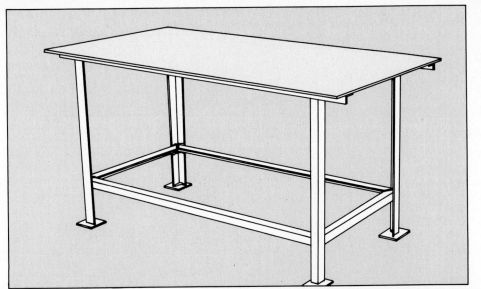

An all-steel workbench. Especially suited to welding, this bench is constructed of 2-by-2-by-¼-inch angle irons with a ¼-inch steel plate on top. Two angle-iron braces welded to the underside of the steel plate provide rigidity and act as abutments to which the angle-iron legs are welded. Four more angle irons, their ends cut at 45° angles, are welded to the legs and can support a shelf. Small squares of steel plate are welded on to form feet for the bench.

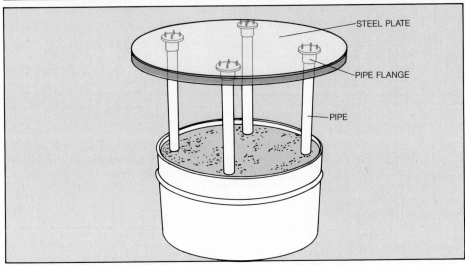

STEEL PLATE

PIPE FLANGE

PIPE

A mighty minibench. This compact, heavy-duty workbench stands up to the rough hammering encountered in metalworking; its concrete base keeps the bench solidly in place and absorbs vibration. Construction starts with a ¼-inch steel plate, attached to 1-inch plywood with flathead wood screws driven through predrilled, countersunk holes. To the underside of the plywood, four pipe flanges are screwed; 2-inch threaded pipes of galvanized steel are screwed into the flanges. The pipes are sunk into concrete that fills a 16-inch-high sawed-off 55-gallon oil drum. For comfortable hammering and bending of cold metal, the top of the bench should be no more than 31 inches off the floor.

Advice on Choosing a Vise

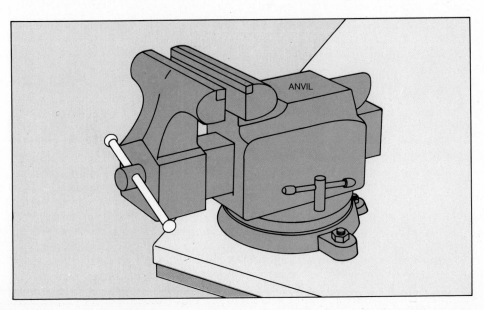

ANVIL

An all-purpose metalworking vise. Often called a machinist's vise, this tool must be strong. The iron body should have 4- to 5-inch jaw faces of hardened steel. A swivel base is useful for positioning work held in the jaws. The small built-in anvil provides a hammering surface.

Install the vise by bolting it to the left front corner of a workbench. To avoid marring metal in the vise jaws, add readymade rubber jaw pads or homemade pads of wood, copper or lead.

11

Specialized Tools for Measuring and Marking

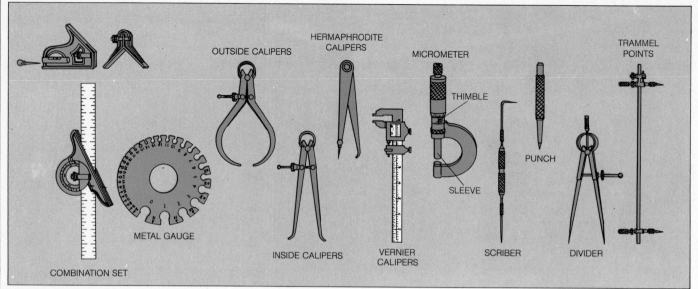

OUTSIDE CALIPERS
HERMAPHRODITE CALIPERS
MICROMETER
TRAMMEL POINTS
THIMBLE
SLEEVE
PUNCH
METAL GAUGE
COMBINATION SET
INSIDE CALIPERS
VERNIER CALIPERS
SCRIBER
DIVIDER

Like fine woodworking, precision metalworking begins with careful measurements. The high cost of metal stock and the relative difficulty with which it is cut make it especially imperative that each cut be right the first time. In addition to the standard measuring tools used by carpenters—steel rules and squares—there are a number of measuring and marking tools designed especially for metalworking.

One particularly versatile tool is the combination set, which is a variation on the carpenter's combination square. It has three interchangeable heads that can be mounted on a single steel rule. One of these heads is used for marking off angles from 0° to 180°, the second for finding the center of a cylindrical shaft, and the third for checking metal corners for squareness.

Because differences in the thickness, called the gauge, of metals are not readily discernible, the tool known by the same name, a metal gauge, is also useful. By inserting metal stock into the slot that fits it best, you can identify the gauge of that piece of metal. Ordinarily, one side of a metal gauge lists gauge numbers, and the other side lists thicknesses in fractions of an inch. The two most widely used gauges are the United States Standard gauge for ferrous metals and the Brown and Sharpe gauge for nonferrous metals.

For measuring very thick stock or irregularly shaped objects, various types of calipers can be employed. Inside and outside calipers are used with a steel rule for simple measurements of width or diameter. The legs of the outside calipers are tightened lightly around the outside of an object; the legs of inside calipers fit inside an opening. The span between the tips of the calipers is then measured with a rule. Vernier calipers combine these two functions and contain a built-in rule. Hermaphrodite calipers—part caliper, part compass—can be used to scribe a line parallel to an irregular edge.

The most precise measuring tool likely to be found in a home metal shop is an outside micrometer. This machinist's tool is used to measure thicknesses or diameters to the nearest thousandth, and sometimes even ten-thousandth, of an inch. The micrometer's jaws are locked around the piece being measured and a reading is taken from two scales, one on the sleeve and one on the thimble that revolves around the sleeve. A third scale, on the arm of the tool, translates the reading into a fraction of an inch.

Because a metal surface is glossy and hard, even marking a legible cutting line can pose a problem. A normal pencil line is usually invisible, and though chalk or a yellow-leaded pencil would be suitable for rough work, the marks they make are inexact and easily rub off. A far better tool for laying out measurements or designs on metal is a scriber, which scratches a fine line on the metal surface. For marking a single point, a hardened-steel punch is useful; the punch is tapped with a ball-peen hammer to leave an imprint on the metal. And to lay out small circles and arcs, use a steel-tipped divider to score the surface of the work.

For scribing larger circles, a pair of trammel points is the most convenient tool. One of the points on this device is stationary; the other point slides along a bar to vary the spacing between points and thus establish the radius for a circle of the desired size.

With some coated metal stocks, such as tin plate or galvanized steel, it is inadvisable to use these scratch-marking techniques. They would expose the underlying layer of metal, allowing it to corrode. To make marks on these materials, first cover the stock with a light coat of steel dye or of copper-sulphate solution. A line lightly scribed through one of these colored coatings is clearly visible, and the metal itself does not have to be scored.

Tools for measuring and marking metal are seemingly endless—and a complete set can be very expensive. To assemble a workable kit for a home shop, begin with a steel rule and square, a combination set, a metal gauge, a scriber, a punch and a steel-tipped divider. Then, when specific projects call for more specialized tools, buy them as they are needed.

Cold Metal Cut Down to Size

It seems paradoxical that a material prized chiefly for its resistance to cutting, breaking and bending should yield so easily to manipulation. Yet with finely honed tools and the proper techniques, metal is surprisingly workable. For projects that involve such commonly used metals as wrought iron or mild steel, the basic dimensioning procedures are sawing, chiseling and filing.

A hacksaw is probably the most familiar metal-cutting tool and also one of the most useful. Its hardened-steel blade will sever most metals found in or around the home; a hacksaw is capable of cutting through metal as thick as one-third the length of its blade.

Hacksaw blades for general use have hardened teeth and are made from molybdenum-, carbon- or tungsten-alloy steel. The critical factors in choosing a blade are the number of teeth per inch and the set of the teeth—the way they are angled on the cutting edge.

For efficient cutting, at least two teeth of a hacksaw blade must always be in contact with the edge of the metal. If the metal is so thin that you cannot keep two teeth on its edge, sandwich it between two thin sheets of plywood for cutting.

Techniques for using a hacksaw are explained on pages 13-15. For safety, avoid excessive pressure, no matter how hard the metal. Too much pressure can cause the blade to snap or to flip out of its kerf; both occurrences can be dangerous.

A number of power tools can be adapted to cutting metal. Electric saber saws, jig saws and band saws can be fitted with special ferrous blades. Power hacksaws are also available. They are excellent tools for straight cuts, but are quite expensive and cannot cut curves.

In fact, no saw can handle all possible cuts in metal. Cuts from the center of a metal plate, for example, are often beyond the reach of a hacksaw blade because the saw's frame gets in the way. For such jobs, either a hacksaw-blade holder without a frame or a cold chisel must be used. The cold chisel has a hardened cutting edge and a handle of slightly softer steel, designed to absorb the blows of a ball-peen hammer.

There are four common kinds of cold chisels, differing in shape according to their purpose (page 15, bottom). They range in width from ⅛ to 1 inch and come in various lengths. For safety and efficiency, a cold chisel must be kept sharp and must be ground to a 60° to 70° angle at its cutting edge.

Be extremely careful to protect your eyes with goggles when using a cold chisel. Leather gloves offer some protection from burrs and jagged edges but may reduce your dexterity in handling thin sheets of metal. A better precaution is to file off the burrs immediately after cutting any metal. Machinist's files (page 16) are used for this purpose. Filing techniques are illustrated on page 17.

For efficiency, metal files must be kept clean. Tap the file handle on the workbench after every few strokes to rid it of metal particles, and brush the file thoroughly with a file card when the file teeth get clogged.

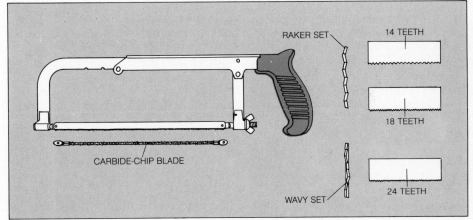

A well-equipped hacksaw. The adjustable C-shaped frame of the hacksaw will hold blades 10 or 12 inches long. The blade snaps over projections on two studs, one at the front of the frame and one held by a wing nut near the handle. To change blades, loosen the wing nut and detach the blade from the studs. To turn the blade sideways within the frame—for long cuts (page 14, top right)—remove the wing nut completely, along with the blade; then turn the studs to the desired position.

Hacksaw blades vary from 4 to 32 teeth per inch. Generally, blades with 4 to 16 teeth are used for soft metals that would clog a blade with finer teeth; blades with 20 to 32 teeth per inch are used to cut hard metals. The standard blade for general-purpose use has 18 teeth per inch.

Coarse-tooth blades usually have a raker set—their teeth are set in a straight line but are bent alternately to either side. The 14- and 18-tooth blades shown in the illustration both have a raker set. Fine-tooth blades usually have a wavy set—their teeth are bent in gently curving lines, as on the 24-tooth blade shown here. This wavy pattern produces a wider kerf, to prevent the blade from binding.

Because of their width, standard hacksaw blades are limited to straight cuts. To cut curves, you need a cylindrical carbide-chip blade, which is less than ¼ inch in diameter. Carbide-chip blades cut by abrasion rather than with sharpened teeth, and they can be used to cut sideways as well as down, producing a wide kerf that allows the blade to follow curved cutting lines.

Straight Cuts Made with a Hacksaw

Cutting across a narrow strip. Clamp the metal stock in a vise, with the scribed cutting line running vertically and close to the jaws of the vise. Place the saw blade on the waste side of the line and pull lightly across the metal until the blade bites into the edge. Then, using both hands, cut along the line; apply light, even pressure on the forward stroke and no pressure on the return. Let the blade do the work; do not try to saw too deeply with each stroke. Near the end of the cut, support the waste metal with one hand to keep it from binding. Shorten the last few cutting strokes until the waste metal is free.

Cutting along a lengthwise edge. Clamp the metal stock in a vise as for a crosswise cut, with the cutting line running vertically. Turn the saw blade perpendicular to the handle of the saw and keep the saw frame horizontal; in this position the frame will not get in the way as the cut deepens. Begin the cut as for the crosswise cut, and again support the waste metal with one hand when the cut is nearly complete.

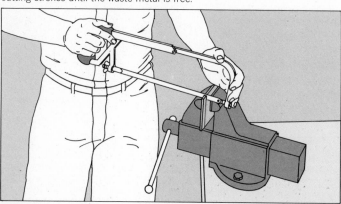

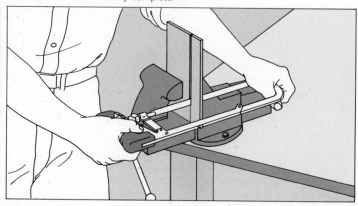

A Notch Shaped with a Hacksaw

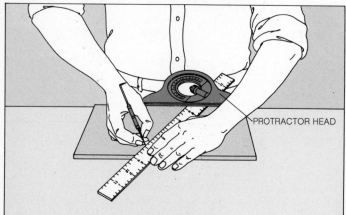

PROTRACTOR HEAD

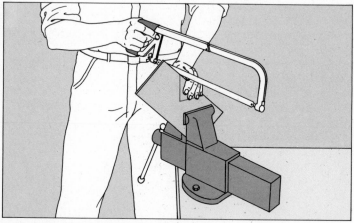

1 **Marking intersecting diagonals.** Use a combination set and a scriber to mark cutting lines for a notch. To locate the lines, first mark the apex of the notch with a punch and ball-peen hammer. Then set the protractor head of the combination set to the desired angle and rest the head against the edge of the metal stock, which should slightly overhang the edge of the workbench. Slide the combination set along the edge of the stock until the rule intersects the punch mark, and scribe the first cutting line. Then, if a change is necessary, adjust the protractor head to the desired angle for the other side of the notch and repeat this marking procedure.

2 **Making the notch cuts.** Clamp the stock in the vise so that one cutting line is vertical and close to the jaws of the vise. To start the cut, steady the side of the blade with your free thumb; otherwise it might slide down the tilted edge of the stock. Once the saw teeth are engaged in the metal, cut with light forward strokes until you reach the intersection point. If necessary, shift the stock in the vise to keep the cutting line close to the jaws. Then turn the stock so that the other cutting line is vertical, and proceed in the same way, again steadying the blade until the teeth are engaged. As you near the intersection, support the V-shaped waste metal with one hand and shorten your cutting strokes.

Using a Hacksaw to Cut a Curve

1 **Marking a curved line.** Set dividers at the radius required for the desired arc and use a punch and a ball-peen hammer to establish a center point for the arc. Place the stationary point of the dividers in that indentation and, holding the top of the dividers loosely with one hand, swing the second point lightly across the metal surface. Be sure to keep the dividers upright, at a right angle to the metal. Use just enough pressure to scribe a visible line.

Clamp the stock in a vise, positioning the cutting line close to the jaws of the vise. This will keep the stock from rocking as you make the cut.

2 **Cutting with a carbide-chip blade.** Using both hands, position the saw blade on the waste side of the cutting line and push the saw slowly forward. Repeat this stroke until the entire width of the blade is buried in the stock, starting each stroke at the front of the blade. Then cut slowly back and forth, applying light, even pressure on both strokes and following the curved cutting line. Reclamp the stock as necessary, to keep the cutting area supported by the jaws of the vise.

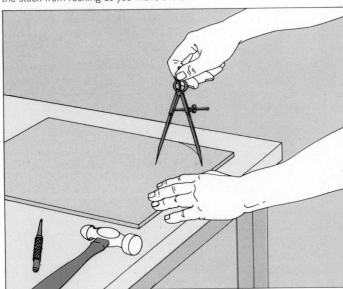

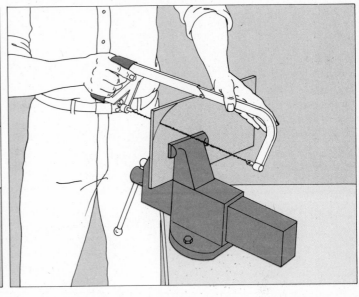

A Variety of Edges for Cold Chisels

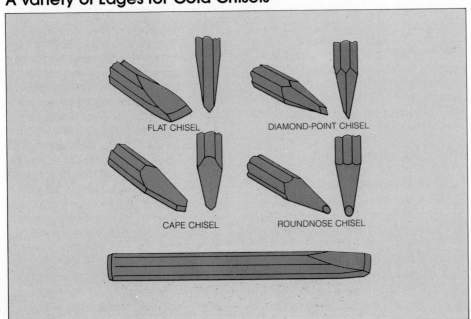

FLAT CHISEL

DIAMOND-POINT CHISEL

CAPE CHISEL

ROUNDNOSE CHISEL

Four types of cold chisels. Cold chisels can be used not only to cut through metal stock, but also to sculpt its surface and to refine its edges. The most common cold-chisel blade has a flat, wedge-shaped tip. It is used for rough shaping, for splitting metal rods, and for shearing the heads off bolts or rivets. A cape chisel is also wedge-shaped but is ground to a much narrower tip; it is used for cutting wedge-shaped grooves or channels. A roundnose chisel is exactly that—its tip is perfectly round. It is useful for rounding the inside corners of a groove or a notch and for cutting flutes. The diamond-point chisel comes to a point. It is used for squaring corners and for cutting narrow lines in metal.

Shearing metal. Clamp the metal stock in a vise, with the cutting line parallel to and just above the top of the jaws. Put on protective goggles, then hold a flat chisel against the cutting line at one end of the stock and tilt the chisel at an angle of 30°. Strike the chisel firmly with a ball-peen hammer. On succeeding cuts, turn the blade slightly toward the previous cut so that the blade acts as a wedge to open the cut. Strike the chisel repeatedly, moving gradually along the top of the vise! Take care to hold the chisel at the proper angle; if the handle is too high, the chisel may damage the vise; if it is too low, the chisel may dent the stock as it cuts it.

Completing a squared notch. After cutting the sides of the notch with a hacksaw, lay the stock flat on a heavy metal plate or on a metal-work bench, and cut the base of the notch with a flat cold chisel. Hold the chisel upright, aligning its blade with one end of the cutting line, and tap lightly with a ball-peen hammer. Repeat this procedure to score the entire line, moving the chisel a little at a time. When the whole line is scored, begin again at one end, using heavier blows this time to sever the metal.

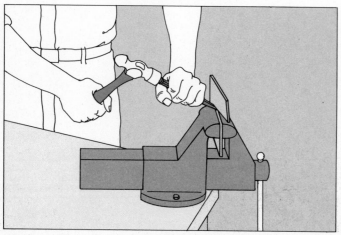

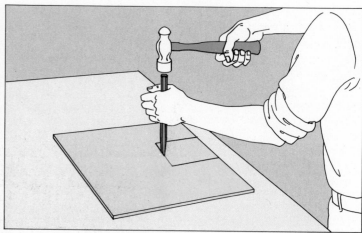

Tools That Shape Metal by Scraping It

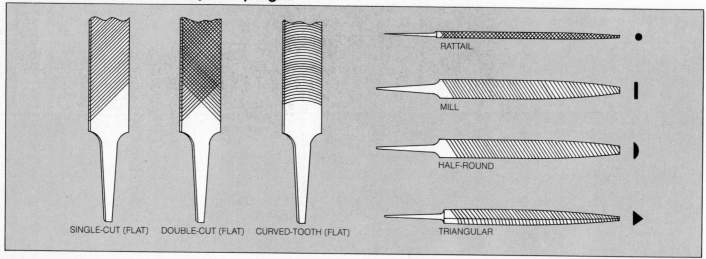

SINGLE-CUT (FLAT) DOUBLE-CUT (FLAT) CURVED-TOOTH (FLAT)

RATTAIL

MILL

HALF-ROUND

TRIANGULAR

Metalworking files. In addition to being available in a variety of shapes—flat, round, half-round and triangular—files are classified according to their cut and degree of coarseness. The cut of a file refers to the pattern of grooves across its face. Single-cut files have parallel gullets running diagonally; they are well suited for fine filing or finishing work. Double-cut files, which have crisscrossed gullets, are twice as abrasive as single-cut files. Curved-tooth files have deep, wide gullets that are cut in an arc pattern; these files are excellent for working on the softer metals, such as aluminum.

In terms of coarseness, files range from bastard files which have deep gullets for rough shaping and surfacing, to second-cut files for general use and to smooth files for finishing. Files range in length from 3 to 20 inches. For general use 8-, 10- and 12-inch files are recommended. For safety, a file should be used only when a handle has been fitted onto the tang.

An assortment of five files will usually suffice for metalworking projects. For flat metal stock, the most useful files are a double-cut 12-inch flat, or hand, file, which is used for rough work, and a single-cut mill file for finishing. A half-round file, double-cut on both its flat and its round sides, is good for rough filing on either flat or concave surfaces. A single- or double-cut round rattail file is best for tight curves or circular openings. For inside corners, a triangular file, double-cut on all three faces, is the best tool.

Techniques to Use for Filing Metal

Cross filing. Clamp the metal stock in a vise, with the edge of the metal as close as possible to the top of the jaws. Lay the file diagonally across the metal edge, and push the handle of the file while using your other hand to guide the blade. For light filing, hold the file point between your thumb and index finger; for rougher, faster filing, put your whole hand on top of the file. Apply pressure only on the forward strokes, then lift the tool to return for the next pass. Work with smooth, regular strokes; avoid rocking the file or chopping on the edge of the metal.

Draw filing. With the metal stock anchored as at left, grip the blade of a mill file with both hands, a few inches apart. Hold the file perpendicular to the stock and level with the surface you are smoothing. Draw the file toward you with a smooth, even motion from the far end of the stock. Shift the blade slightly between strokes so that you are always working with a clear surface of the file. If the blade gets clogged, stop and clean it with a file card.

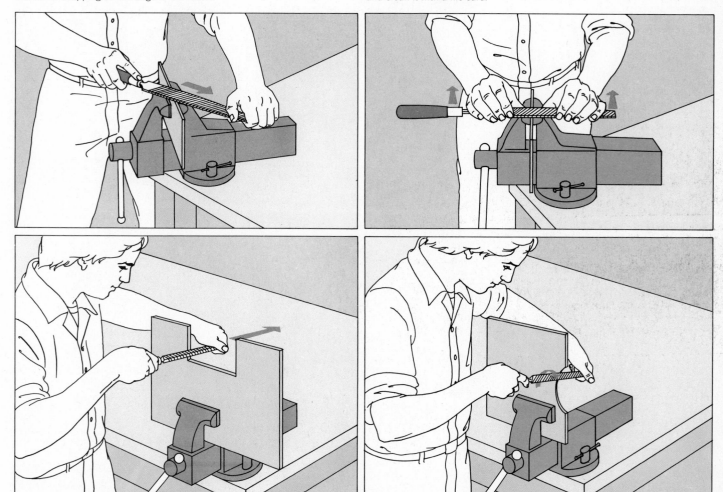

Filing inside corners. Clamp the stock in a vise in a position that allows you to work comfortably with both hands on the file. Rest one face of a triangular file against one side of the inside corner. Push the file forward while you guide it away from the corner. File with smooth forward strokes, returning the file each time to the starting position. Smooth one side of the corner at a time. Avoid pressing down into the corner because pressure might disfigure the angle. Also take care to hold the face of the file perpendicular to the edge you are smoothing.

Filing a curve. Clamp the stock in a vise with the curved edge vertical, and smooth the edge with the rounded face of a half-round file. Grasp the point of the file between your thumb and index finger, with your thumb on top. File the curve on your forward strokes, giving the blade a clockwise half twist as it moves forward. Turn the work in the vise as often as necessary to make smooth, even strokes.

Shaping with Power Grinders

For shaping metal edges and smoothing welded joints, a power grinder—either a bench grinder or a portable, hand-held sander-grinder—is indispensable. The bench grinder is ideal for rounding off corners of hard metals and removing burrs from cut edges; it is the better choice for shaping small iron or steel objects. The portable power grinder excels at smoothing wide areas of flat metal, especially around welds. But you have no choice for grinding nonferrous metals safely. Because a bench grinder's stone wheel collects fragments of such metals and hurls them back at you, you must use a portable grinder fitted with an emery disk or a special ferrous disk.

With either power grinder, observe these safety precautions: Stop grinding if the metal edge being ground begins to turn blue—this means the metal is dangerously overheated. Quench the workpiece frequently. Hold or clamp the metal firmly, especially while grinding the end of a long object on a bench grinder. In a portable grinder, insist on two important safety features: an on-off trigger that turns the machine off when released, and either a double-insulated or a three-pronged grounded electric plug.

Transforming a Square Corner into a Curve

1 **Marking the curve.** After scribing the desired arc on the metal to be ground, make the arc more visible by punching holes along it. Use a center punch and a ball-peen hammer, spacing the punch marks about ⅛ inch apart.

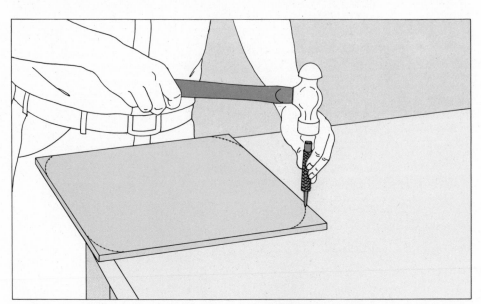

2 **Grinding the arc.** Set the tool rest at a right angle to the center of the wheel and ⅛ inch from it. With the grinder on, place the metal on the tool rest and bring the corner into light contact with the face of the wheel. Rotate the corner slowly in a wide, semicircular motion, moving the metal continuously back and forth over the wheel. To be sure of obtaining the correct radius, do not grind beyond the line of punched holes. Quench frequently to prevent overheating.

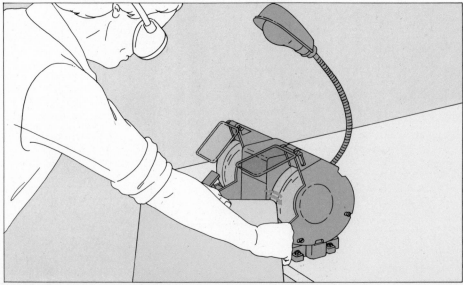

Beveled Edges Shaped on a Bench Grinder

Beveling a pipe. With the grinder turned on, hold the section of pipe at an acute angle to the wheel. Rest the bottom of the pipe end to be beveled on the tool rest, and bring one edge into contact with the wheel as it spins. Rotate the pipe slowly clockwise across the surface of the wheel. Quench the pipe frequently in the waterpot of the grinder while you work.

Beveling a flat edge. Set the tool rest at the desired angle. With the grinder on, place the metal on the tool rest and bring the edge lightly against the wheel. Slide the edge from side to side on the tool rest as you work. Check the angle with a protractor, and quench the edge often.

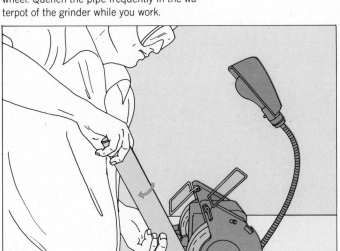

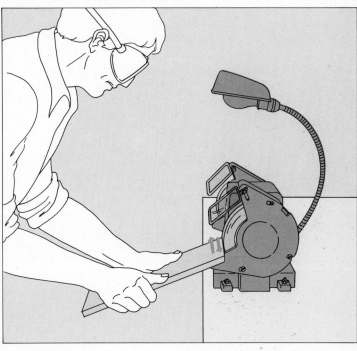

Using a Portable Grinder to Dress a Weld

Using a sander-grinder. Secure the welded sheet to the bench with clamps. Turn on the portable grinder, and bring the leading edge of the grinding wheel into contact with the weld. Tilt the grinder so that only the front edge of the wheel is touching the weld. Run the wheel lightly over the joint to remove any irregularities and smooth the surface of the metal.

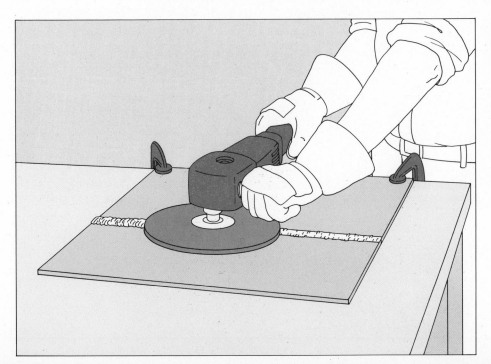

Bends and Twists with Leverage and Muscle

Despite its strength, up to a certain point metal can be bent without heat by means of mechanical leverage; it may even look better than if heated. Curves made in cold metal, for instance—such as the spiral twists of a stair railing—tend to be smoother, since heated metal kinks more readily than cold metal.

Although virtually any kind of metal can be bent cold, the more pliable metals are the easiest to work (*page 9*). Hard metals are more likely to crack. Metals most commonly bent while cold are mild steel, aluminum and copper—usually available in strips and in round or square rods, at hardware stores and at metal-supply shops. Any metal strip that is to be bent cold should be no more than ¼ inch thick and no more than 1½ inches wide; larger strips are usually too rigid for cold bending. However, metal rods as thick as ⅜ inch can be bent.

Thin tubing can also be bent cold, for plumbing and electrical work or for furniture. To avoid turning the tube so sharply that its inner wall collapses or becomes crimped, use aluminum, copper or steel tubing, such as electrical conduit,

with walls no thicker than 1/16 inch. For shaping soft copper tubing, a set of tube-bending springs ranging from ¼ inch to ⅝ inch in diameter is helpful. These 1-foot-long springs fit snugly on the outside of the tube, distributing the bending force along the spring's length to prevent the tube from kinking. For very stiff tubing, rent a conduit bender from an electrical-supply store. This easy-to-use jig will form obtuse angles up to 90°.

Bending metal rods and strips requires only a few tools. A metalworking vise is essential, to hold the work and act as a fulcrum. An ideal vise will open up to 6 inches, has a swivel base to allow a variety of work angles, and has smooth jaws so that the metal is not scored or scratched. To hold pipe and other cylindrical objects, a vise with a V groove in one jaw works best. Also useful is an anvil for hammering metal.

To increase your leverage ,when you bend cold metal, invest in a pipe wrench; for twisting, rather than bending (*page 23*), you will need a pair of such wrenches. Pad the metal with masking tape, if necessary, to protect it from the serrated

jaws of the wrenches. Also for added leverage, keep an assortment of metal pipes, with large and small diameters, to use as extensions that you can slip over the rods, strips or tubes you are bending. For scroll bending, there is a special jig with anchored pins that pinch the metal strap as you apply pressure; or you can make your own jig, as shown on page 22.

For driving cold metal around a form and for flattening bumps and bends, there are hammers and sledges ranging in weight from a light 2-ounce ball-peen hammer to a 3-pound small sledge. Use the heaviest tool that you can comfortably handle; its weight will do a large part of the work.

Whenever you bend curves in cold metal, plan ahead by making a full-sized drawing to use as a guide. To make a drawing for a large object, you may need to draw a small sketch and then enlarge it part by part.

Work gradually, and expect some spring-back as you pull and push the metal into shape. Always wear heavy gloves to protect your hands from sharp edges and errant hammer blows.

Simple Angled Bends

1 **Making a simple bend.** Using a scratch awl or a triangular file, mark the bend line. If the length of the bent strip must be precise, take the bend itself into account—the bend will shorten the strip along the underside and lengthen it along the top by half the metal's thickness. Clamp the metal in a vise, lining up the bend line with the edge of the vise jaws, and pull the free end of the strip toward you. For added leverage, slide a two-foot length of pipe over the free end of the metal strip, and pull on the pipe.

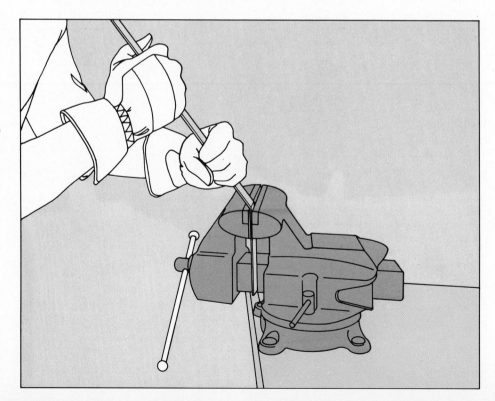

2 **Squaring off a corner.** Unclamp the bent metal and turn it sideways in the vise, with the rounded corner braced against a vise jaw. Then, with a sledge, strike the metal at the corner to create a sharp 90° bend.

To make an acute angle—one sharper than 90°—slide the metal out of the vise partway and reclamp it; then slip a pipe over the free end of the metal and pull the pipe toward the vise. Check the angle with a protractor, and bend the metal in either direction as necessary.

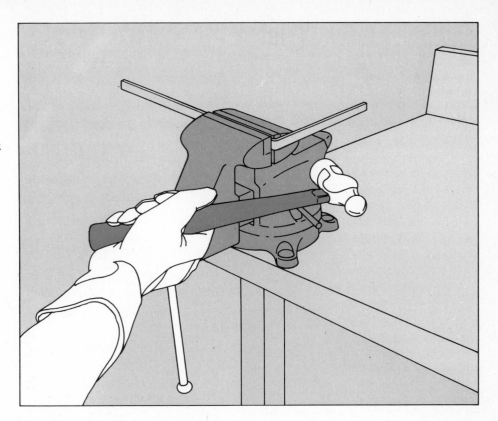

Laying Out Curves on a Template

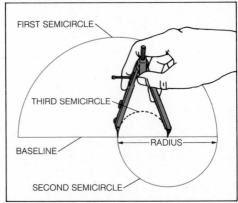

FIRST SEMICIRCLE

THIRD SEMICIRCLE

BASELINE

RADIUS

SECOND SEMICIRCLE

Laying out a scroll. To lay out a scroll, first make a baseline that will form the largest diameter of the scroll. Find the midpoint of the baseline and use a compass (or a nail, string and pencil) to draw a semicircle. Then find the midpoint of the semicircle's radius; continue the scroll line with a second semicircle, making it half the size of the first. Continue to add semicircles of decreasing size until you have the number of turns you want in the scroll.

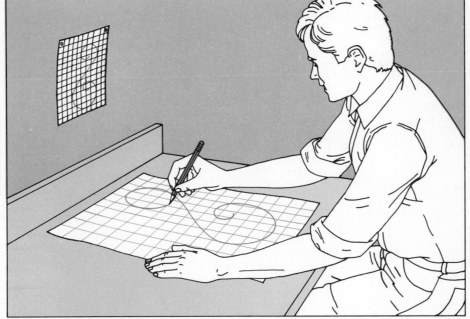

Enlarging a small sketch. Using a sheet of ¼-inch grid paper, draw a small sketch of the metal shape you are planning. Measure the longest dimension of the form as you have sketched it, and divide this number into the longest dimension desired for the enlarged sketch. This gives the multiple of the large sketch as compared with the small. Multiply this figure by ¼ inch to get the size of the grid squares needed for the larger sketch. Lay out the large grid on a piece of heavy wrapping paper, and transfer the small sketch to the large grid by redrawing each section of the small sketch, box by box, on the corresponding squares on the large grid. Then smooth out the curves of the large pattern, using a broad-tipped felt marking pen.

Hand-cut Curves and Scrolls

Forming a curve. Cut a section of strap or rod to the length needed for the finished piece. To determine this length, bend a wire along the contours of the paper template, then straighten the wire and measure it. Using the template, find where the curve will start and end, and mark these points on the workpiece with a pencil.

Clamp the work in a vise between a vise jaw and a pipe that has an outside diameter about the same as the inside diameter of the curve. Then bend the metal toward you until its shape matches the template. For a longer, gentler curve, bend the metal in several places in succession, feeding the metal farther down into the vise for each bend you make.

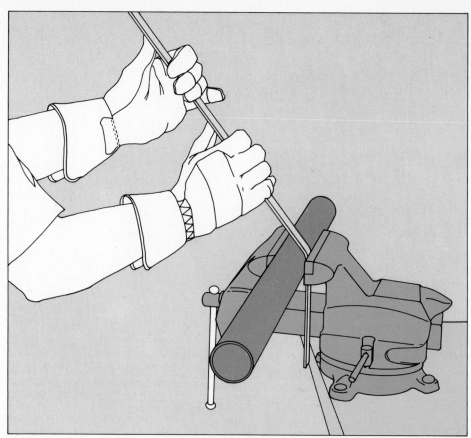

Finishing a scroll. To bend the end of a metal strap into a scroll, clamp a special scroll-bending jig in a vise and slide the strap between the pins of the jig; the pins should be placed in holes close to the strap. Feed the strap through the jig, bending the strap to match the scroll shape on your template.

You can make your own scroll-bending jig by bending a ⅜-inch mild-steel rod into a U shape *(inset)*. To do this, first bend the rod ends at an acute angle, then finish the bend by squeezing the legs of the U in a vise. Leave a space between the legs equal to the thickness of the metal strap you will bend. Cut excess rod from the jig with a hacksaw; jig ends should protrude 1¼ inches above the strap when one inch of the U-shaped end is clamped in the vise.

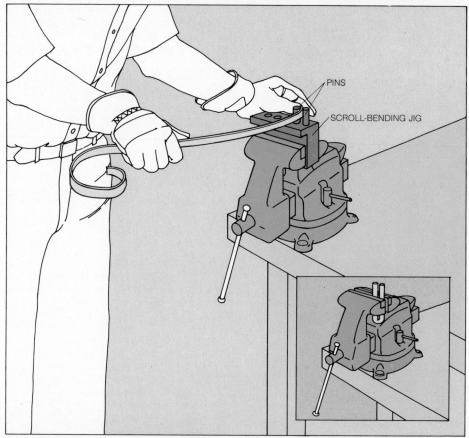

PINS

SCROLL-BENDING JIG

How to Make Symmetrical Twists in Cold Straps

Using pipe wrenches for leverage. Cut a strap or rod at least 1 inch longer than the desired finished length, and clamp one end in the vise. Then form a twist handle on the free end with two large pipe wrenches, tightly clamped to the metal so that they project in opposite directions, perpendicular to the strap. To protect the metal from scratches, pad it with masking tape before tightening the wrench jaws.

Slowly rotate the wrenches until the twists, which will automatically be evenly spaced, develop along the length of the metal. Use a hacksaw to cut the metal to the exact length needed.

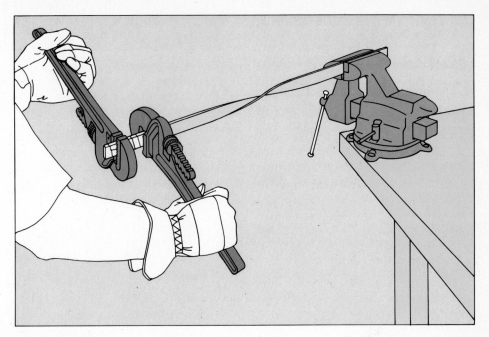

Tubes and Conduit Bent without Kinking

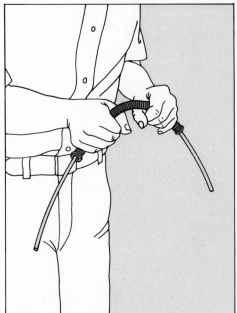

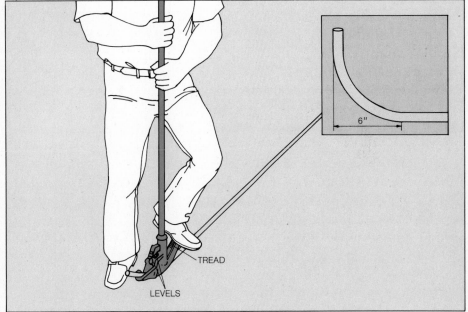

Using a bending spring. If you are working with thin-walled tubing—thinner than $1/16$ inch—calculate where the bend will be located and mark the end points on the tube with a pencil. Then slide the tubing into the flared end of a bending spring and pull it through; choose a spring that fits snugly over the area to be bent.

Bend the tube by hand, holding it at the pencil marks. Or clamp one end in a vise and pull downward to make the bend. As a rule, the bend should not exceed 90°, although very thin tubing may be bent at a sharper angle without kinking. Pull the spring off by grasping the flared end.

Using a conduit bender. Mark the beginning and end of the bend, lay the tubing on the ground and insert one end of the tubing into a conduit bender; align the beginning mark with the arrow on the bender. Step on the tread and pull on the handle. The metal can be bent at 45° or 90° over a distance of 6 inches *(inset)*; the spirit levels indicate at what angle the tubing is bent. If the bender you are using is not equipped with spirit levels, pull the handle to a vertical position for a 45° bend, or to an angle of 45° to the ground for a 90° turn.

For compound bend, make the first bend and remove the tubing from the bender. Turn the bender upside down so that its handle rests on the ground. Insert the tubing so that the arrow aligns with the end of the first bend, and pull down on the tubing to make the second bend. You may need a helper to steady the bender.

High-Precision Holes Drilled with Power Tools

Homeowners often need to make holes in metal to accommodate fasteners and other mechanical parts that require an opening of an exact size. Although an ordinary electric hand drill *(page 26)* bores a hole that is precise enough for some of these needs, the tool of choice for more professional work is the drill press, a machine that combines a powerful, variable-speed drill with a secure, adjustable work surface. The drill's speed is changed by moving a motor-driven belt from one pulley level to another. In this way, you can vary the torque, or turning force, of the drill to suit the hardness of the metal.

With any type of drill, the size and shape of the hole you make are determined by the drill bit you use. A straight (but sometimes inexact) hole is made with a common twist bit—a pointed metal cylinder with a helical channel that spirals down the shaft of the bit. A twist bit bores into the metal and carries the cut chips up the channel and out of the

hole. In soft sheet metals such as aluminum or copper, such a bit often cuts a ragged hole; for these metals you can use a sheet-metal bit, which has a point flanked by two cutting flanges.

Always use high-speed drill bits for making holes in metal. Fashioned of the hardest steel, such bits range in diameter from less than 1/64 inch up to 1 inch. Sizes are designated in different ways: by letters from A to Z, by wire-gauge sizes, in millimeters, in inches or by numbers. To make holes larger than 1 inch, you can fit the drill with a hole saw—a toothed cylinder that cuts holes up to 6 inches in diameter and up to two thirds the depth of the hole saw itself. You can also use a hole saw to make shallow holes that will conceal the heads of such fasteners as bolts, rivets and screws.

For perfectly precise holes up to 1½ inches, you will need to ream the hole after you drill it. Reaming can be done by hand or machine. Hand reamers are straight bits with four or more lengthwise

cutting edges that gradually pare away the inside of the hole as you rotate the reamer. Adjustable hand reamers are available, but they are less exact than fixed-size reamers. Machine reamers fit in a drill press.

Any time you drill a hole, you will need to use a special metal-cutting fluid that reduces friction and cools the bit as it turns. You will also need clamps and vises to hold the work exactly where you want it and to prevent it from being wrenched from your grip. To mark the place where you will drill, you should use a center punch to make a small dimple for the drill point. All of these supplies can be found at most hardware stores.

If the precision of a drill press is not needed, a heavy-duty electric hand drill can be used; it has the advantage of being easily transported to the job site. But unless it is a variable-speed drill, it can be slowed for metalwork only by a technique known as feathering—pressing the trigger in repeated short bursts.

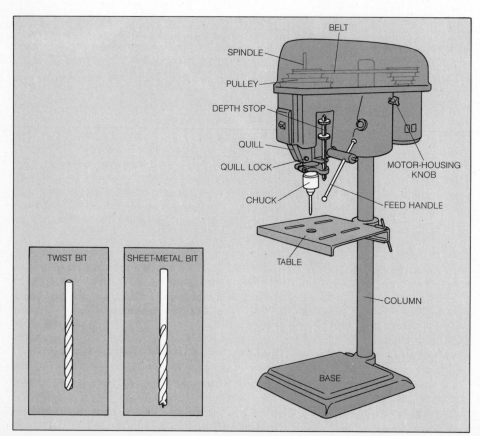

TWIST BIT

SHEET-METAL BIT

BELT

SPINDLE

PULLEY

DEPTH STOP

QUILL

QUILL LOCK

CHUCK

TABLE

MOTOR-HOUSING KNOB

FEED HANDLE

COLUMN

BASE

A Drill Press and Bits for Work with Metal

Anatomy of a drill press. Sold either as a full-sized floor model or as a bench model with a shorter column, a drill press consists of an adjustable table, plus a motor-driven spindle and chuck that lower the spinning drill bit into the metal. The head houses a motor connected to the spindle with four-level pulleys and a belt.

The drill bit is gripped by the jaws of the chuck. The bit is lowered by means of a feed handle; the operator can control the hole's depth either by setting the depth stop or by raising or lowering the table. The spindle, inside a sleeve called the quill, is retracted into the head when not is use. Many drill presses have a quill lock to hold the quill down while you set up the work.

Two kinds of drill bits are used for metal. The high-speed twist bit used for drilling metal thicker than ¼ inch *(inset, far left)* has a shank, a helical channel called a flute that carries drilled metal out of the hole, and a land—the untooled section of the shank, rimmed with a cutting edge beside the flute. The flat cutting tip is called the web. A sheet-metal bit *(inset, near left)* cuts a clean edge around a hole in thin metal, thus preventing any tearing of the metal.

Choosing the Right Drill Speed for the Job

Diameter	Cast iron, hard steel	Mild steel	Aluminum, brass, bronze
⅛ in.	2,100	3,050	6,500
¼ in.	1,100	1,500	4,600
⅓ in.	700	1,000	3,150
½ in.	500	750	2,300
1 in.	250	400	1,000

Approximate speeds in rpm's. Choose the most effective drill speed, expressed in revolutions per minute (rpm), by finding the hole diameter in the left-hand column and the metal you are drilling in one of the three right-hand columns. Depending on the metal and the diameter, the proper drilling speed varies from 250 rpm for a 1-inch hole drilled in cast iron to about 6,500 rpm for a ⅛-inch hole drilled in aluminum. These figures are approximate and may not correspond exactly to the speeds that are recommended by the manufacturer of your drill press. In general, the smaller the bit and the softer the metal, the faster the speed you will need.

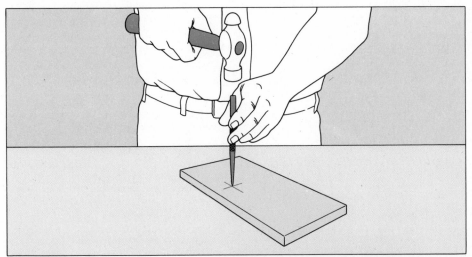

Setting Up the Work for Accurate Drilling

1 **Marking the hole.** To locate the hole, use a ruler and a scriber *(page 12)* to draw two short lines intersecting at right angles at the center of the hole. To keep the bit from wandering, make a tiny dent at the center point, using a center punch and a ball-peen hammer.

Determine the necessary drill speed, then set the drill to operate at that speed.

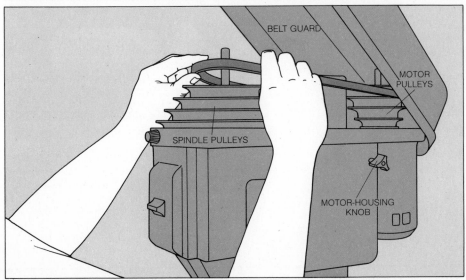

BELT GUARD

MOTOR PULLEYS

SPINDLE PULLEYS

MOTOR-HOUSING KNOB

2 **Adjusting the drill speed.** Open the belt guard and release the tension on the pulleys by unscrewing the motor-housing knob. To change speeds, push the motor frame forward and slip the belt from one pulley level to another, according to the speed ratings printed on the nameplate of the drill press or listed in the owner's manual. The slowest speeds are obtained at the lowest tier of pulleys, with the belt looped between the smallest motor pulley and the largest spindle pulley. Conversely, the fastest speed is obtained when the belt is looped around the highest pulleys.

Make sure the belt is horizontal between the pulleys. Then push the motor back to its original position and tighten the motor-housing knob.

3 **Drilling a hole.** Put the drill bit into the chuck and tighten the chuck. Adjust the drill press for the depth of the hole by lowering the bit alongside the work and turning the depth stop to the desired point on the calibrated stop rod. Then raise the bit just enough to slide the work under it, using the quill lock to hold the bit so that you can position the punched hole exactly under the point. Clamp the work well with C clamps.

Loosen the quill lock and turn on the power to the drill press. Place a drop of cutting fluid on the hole you punched previously, pull on the feed lever and begin drilling. Apply even pressure; use a brush to remove chips and shavings as they collect, adding more cutting fluid as you work. Smoke may begin to drift out of the bored hole; if it does, ease up on the feed handle and check the color of the metal chips. They should be silver or straw yellow; if they are bluish, the metal is overheating, and you should add more cutting fluid or reduce the speed of the drill press. When you finish the hole, release the feed handle slowly, then turn off the power.

For holes ⅜ inch in diameter or larger, drill a pilot hole first, to the depth of the final hole. The pilot hole should be slightly larger than the web of the bit you will use to drill the final hole.

For odd-shaped work, clamp the work in a drill-press vise *(inset, left)* and clamp the vise to the table, using C clamps or vise bolts that fasten through the slots in the table. Some drill-press vises have a V-grooved jaw for cylinders. Or use a V block *(inset, right)* to hold the cylinder, clamping the block in the drill-press vise.

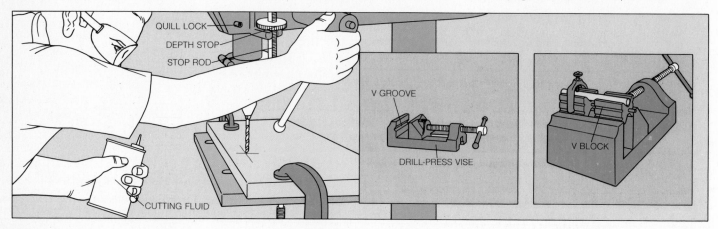

QUILL LOCK
DEPTH STOP
STOP ROD
CUTTING FLUID
V GROOVE
DRILL-PRESS VISE
V BLOCK

Portable-Drill Precision

Holding the drill. Clamp the work in a vise or to a bench. Then, with the power to the drill off, place the tip of the bit in the punched starting hole. To enlarge the starting hole, rotate the chuck by hand several times, pressing down on the bit. Apply cutting fluid, turn on the power and hold the drill body steady with your left hand while pushing with your right as the drill speeds up. If possible, set an upright try square beside the drill to help you align the drill bit vertically. If you are not using a variable-speed drill, vary the speed by feathering the drill—intermittently squeezing the trigger and releasing it. Ease up on the pressure as you reach the bottom of the hole, but let the bit continue spinning as you remove it from the hole.

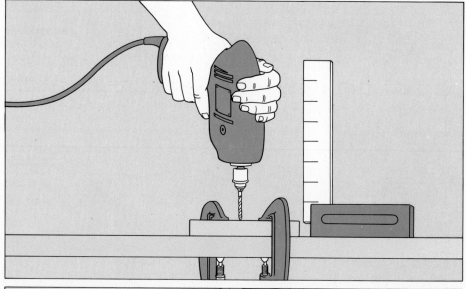

Correcting a drifting bit. Use a cold chisel and a ball-peen hammer to make a groove from the middle of an off-center hole to the intended center. If the metal is soft or the hole is smaller than ¼ inch in diameter, scratch the groove with a half-round chisel. Then use the groove to guide the bit's point back to the original center. Caution: This works only for a twist bit, which bores with its tip; it will not work for a sheet-metal bit, which cuts with its side edges *(page 24)*.

Using a Round Saw to Cut Large Holes

A hole saw for large holes. Fit the hole saw onto its mandrel *(inset)* and tighten the mandrel in the chuck of the drill press. Reduce the speed of the drill to half the speed recommended for holes up to 1 inch *(page 25)*, or to the slowest possible speed for larger holes. Use extra cutting fluid while cutting the hole.

To prevent sheet metal from tearing or buckling when you cut it with a hole saw, sandwich the workpiece between two sheets of ½-inch plywood. Cut access holes in the plywood that are larger than the hole you plan to drill in the metal, using an oversized hole saw. Center the work under the drill, and clamp the whole assembly to the table; then cut the hole in the metal.

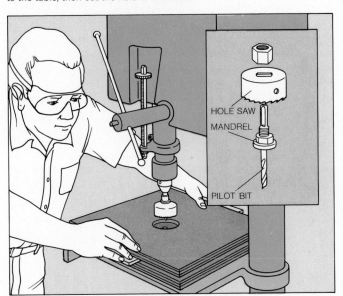

Flush Fasteners with Countersinking

Holes for screwheads. To widen the top of a hole to accommodate a tapered screwhead, fit a cone-shaped countersinking bit into the chuck of a drill press or a hand drill. Drill at the slowest possible speed, and apply cutting fluid liberally. As you drill, check the circumference of the hole by setting an upside-down screwhead over the hole. The two should match perfectly, so that the screw will be flush with the surface of the metal when it is in place *(inset)*.

To inset boltheads, make a cylindrical, or counterbored, hole with a counterbore bit ¹⁄₁₆ inch larger than the bolthead. Make the hole deep enough that the top of the bolt is flush with the metal surface when it is in place *(inset)*.

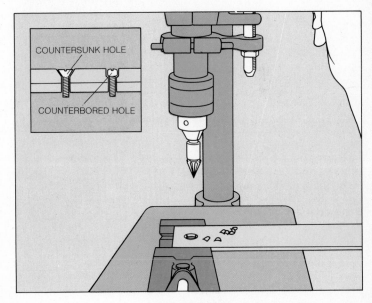

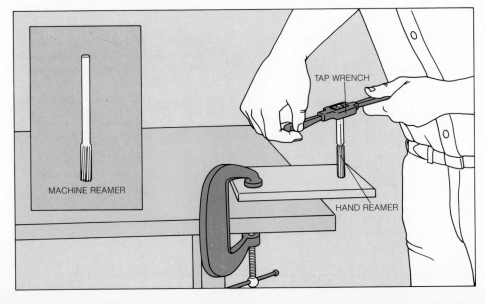

For Maximum Precision, Reaming a Drilled Hole

Using a reamer. If you plan to use a reamer for extra precision, drill the hole ¹⁄₆₄ inch narrower than it will be when finished. To center the reamer, deburr the hole by countersinking it slightly. Select a hand reamer of the appropriate size, and attach a tap wrench to it by tightening the wrench's handle. Lubricate the hole with cutting fluid, insert the reamer in the hole and turn the reamer clockwise, working slowly and evenly with slight pressure, until it can go no farther. Then twist the reamer out of the hole, still turning it clockwise.

To ream a hole with a drill press, use a spiral-flute machine reamer *(inset)*. Attach the machine reamer, and finish the hole with the reamer, using the slowest speed possible.

Hand-cut Threads Made with Taps and Dies

Threading is one of the classic ways to join metal to metal and metal to wood. Based on Archimedes' famous screw, this ingenious fastening method uses matched sets of spiraling grooves to interlock adjoining parts. Once threading was a handicraft; each craftsman cut threads with tools of his own design—which meant that few threaded parts were interchangeable. Today, threads are cut with high-carbon-steel taps and dies that come in standardized sizes. The taps cut threads inside a hole; the dies thread the outside of pipes or rods.

Tap and die sizes are based on one of two systems. The most common in the United States is the American National Thread System, adopted in 1911. In this system, thread sizes are specified as either NC, National Coarse, or NF, National Fine. The former is for general-purpose use; the latter, with more threads per inch, is for precision assemblies. The thread sizes, stamped on the tap or die, indicate the outside, or major, diameter of the thread, the number of threads per inch, and whether the threads are National Coarse or National Fine.

When the outside diameter is less than ¼ inch, taps and dies are marked with a gauge number, corresponding to the gauges of machine screws. For example, a tap stamped 8-32NC will cut threads for a No. 8 machine screw with 32 threads per inch in the National Coarse designation. A die stamped ¼-28NF will cut 28 threads per inch on a ¼-inch-diameter rod in the National Fine designation.

In the other system, which uses metric measurements, the designations are slightly different. The outside diameter is given in millimeters, and so is the thread pitch (right), which corresponds to the threads-per-inch designation of the American National system. In addition, every metric tap or die bears a class number from 1 to 3, indicating tightness of fit; Class 1 is loose, Class 3 is close, or tight. In this system, tightness of fit is analogous to National Coarse and National Fine, in that it makes distinctions between precise and less precise work.

When you are cutting threads to match those on an existing screw, bolt or nut, you will need to measure the number of threads on the fastener with a screw-pitch gauge in order to select the correct tap or die. The gauge has blades toothed to fit between the threads on the existing fastener. One end of the gauge has blades corresponding to National Coarse, the other side to National Fine.

Before tapping a hole for a screw or a bolt, you may have to drill the actual hole (page 24). This hole must correspond to the size of the tap and must be made with a special tap drill bit. Most tap-and-drill sets contain a tap drill chart to help you select the right drill bit; the charts are available in hardware stores. The chart will indicate, for example, that you would need a No. 29 bit for a hole to accommodate an 8-32NC tap.

If you have never used taps or dies before, practice on a piece of scrap metal. The keys to cutting clean, accurate threads are to work with sharp taps and dies, and to keep the work square and well lubricated if lubrication is called for. When tapping, use a try square as a guide to keep threads straight; when cutting with a die, use the guide on the diestock. You should lubricate the tools and work area liberally with the appropriate cutting fluid when you are working with steel, copper, bronze or aluminum; brass and cast iron are cut dry.

When tapping, work slowly; taps are brittle and sometimes break. If this happens, you may be able to remove the broken pieces with a sharp tool such as a scribe, and start over with a new tap. But in most cases you will have to scrap the job. Similarly, if you cut ragged threads, you may be able to rethread the hole or rod—but generally the chances of correcting the damage are slim.

Thread cutting requires some precautions, since it produces sharp metal chips. Wear goggles at all times, and use a brush or a cloth to remove the chips from the threads and work surface. Make sure taps and dies are clamped securely. Taps are normally held in wrenches and are turned by hand. Dies are held in a special tool accessory called a diestock.

The Profile of a Thread

A continuous cut with many parts. The spiral-shaped groove that a thread cuts inside a hole or around the outside of a rod or pipe has its own special nomenclature. Its outside diameter, called the major diameter, is the largest span across the screw thread; it is the measurement that determines the width of the tap or die used in cutting. The minor diameter, sometimes called the root diameter, is the shortest diameter across the screw thread; it determines the size of tap drill bits, which should be slightly larger than the minor diameter of a thread. The crest is the peaked top formed by the two sloping sides of the threads; the root is the valley at the bottom. The thread angle is the angle of the sloping sides, which in the American National Thread System is always 60°. The pitch is the distance between the two crests of the thread; it is commonly expressed as a fraction based on the number of threads per inch—a screw with eight threads per inch, for example, would have a pitch of ⅛. Thread depth is the distance between the crest and the root, measured along an imaginary line bisecting the angle between two adjacent crests and running at right angles to the axis of the cylinder—either a rod or a hole—into which the thread is cut.

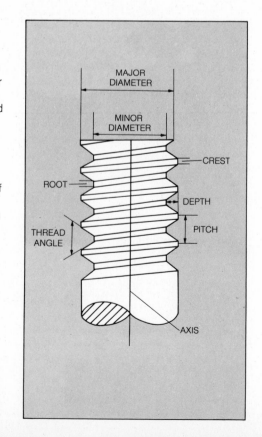

Tools for cutting threads. Standard taps for cutting threads on the inside of holes come in three styles, each designed for a specific purpose. A taper tap, or starting tap, used to start the threading process, tapers back from the tip for a distance of five to ten threads; the tapered tip aligns the tap in the hole during the initial stages of cutting. A plug tap tapers back only three or four threads and offers a greater cutting surface; it is often used after the threading pattern is established. A bottoming tap, with no taper at all, is used to carry the threading to the bottom of a blind hole—a hole that does not go all the way through the metal.

A special pipe tap, wider in diameter than standard taps and used for threading the inside of pipes, tapers all along its length. It produces a tapered thread, needed for a tight fit between sections of pipe to carry water, steam or gas. (Pipe taps for electrical conduit and for threading to connectors are straight.) Pipe taps are marked with the outside pipe diameter and NPT (National Pipe Thread). Taps are turned with tap wrenches—a T-handle wrench for smaller taps, a bar wrench for larger ones.

Dies are commonly of two kinds, hexagonal solid and round adjustable. There is a split on the adjustable die that can be widened or narrowed by means of a screw, for making fine adjustments within a given size—a useful feature in rethreading when you need a closer or a looser fit. On one side of a die, the opening is wider for one or two threads, so that the die can be firmly seated over the end of the rod at the beginning of the cut. Most pipe dies, like pipe taps, taper continuously from one side to the other and are stamped with the size of the pipe rather than with the size of the thread. Dies are held by means of a diestock, which usually has a guide for lining up the die with the pipe or rod, to ensure that the cut will be straight.

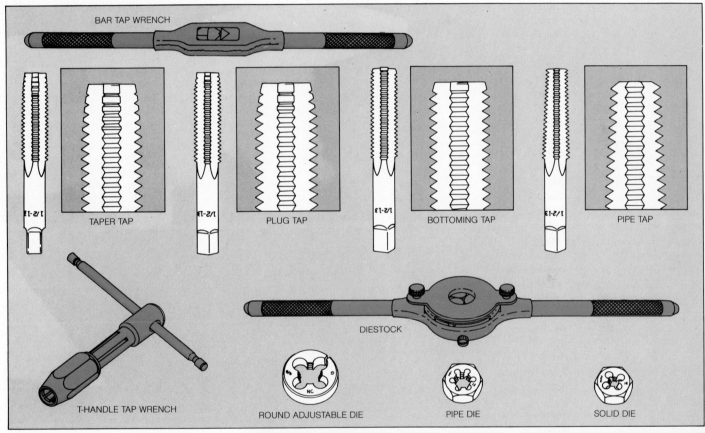

BAR TAP WRENCH

TAPER TAP   PLUG TAP   BOTTOMING TAP   PIPE TAP

DIESTOCK

T-HANDLE TAP WRENCH   ROUND ADJUSTABLE DIE   PIPE DIE   SOLID DIE

A handy measure for matching threads. To determine the proper tap size for threading a hole to match a bolt or screw, hold different blades of a screw-pitch gauge against the threads of the fastener until one blade fits. The number stamped on the blade is the number of threads per inch. Then measure the major diameter of the threads with calipers. The two numbers combined indicate the correct tap size for that particular bolt or screw.

Repeat this procedure to determine the proper die size for cutting threads on a rod or pipe to match the threads of a nut or a threaded flange.

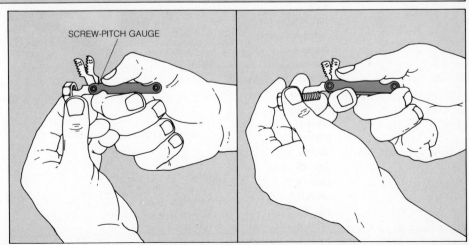

SCREW-PITCH GAUGE

Threading a Hole with a Tap

1 Starting the threads. Clamp the metal work-piece in a vise, with the previously drilled hole in an upright position. Place a taper tap, held in a tap wrench, directly over the hole. To anchor the tap in the wrench, unscrew the chuck or the handle—depending on whether it is a T-handle wrench or a bar wrench—and insert the square end of the tap; tighten the wrench against the tap until the latter is secure.

Squirt cutting fluid *(page 24)* on the end of the tap, and spread it into the hole with a small brush. Then, with the tap lined up with the hole, grasp the wrench with one hand and press down, turning the tap clockwise. Maintain a steady pressure, and give the tap one full turn.

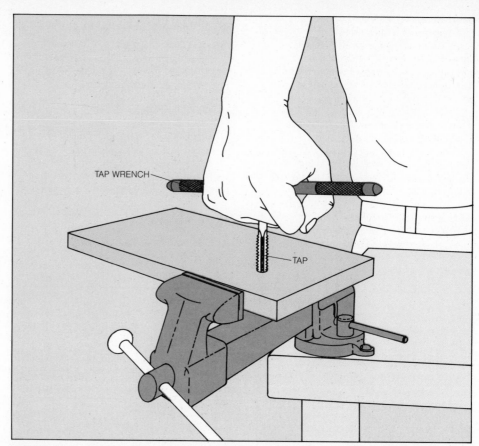

TAP WRENCH

TAP

2 Checking the threads for alignment. After you have cut the first thread, stand a try square on end about an inch away from the tap, positioning it so that the tap handle will touch the square on the next quarter turn. Grasping the wrench with both hands, step back and sight along the tap and square, to check whether the tap is vertical. If tap and square are not in alignment, unscrew the tap and straighten it.

When you are satisfied that tap and square line up in this first position, give the tap a quarter turn and move the square a quarter turn beyond it. Once again sight along them to make sure the tap is straight, adjusting it again if necessary. Repeat this procedure two more times until you have completed one full revolution of the tap and have squared it at every quarter turn.

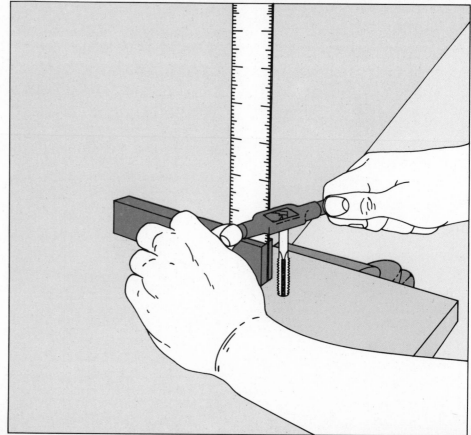

3 Completing the threads. When the tap is properly aligned, continue screwing it into the hole steadily and slowly. Do not use pressure; once engaged, the tap is drawn into the hole by its own cutting action. After every two full turns, back up the tap a quarter turn or half turn to snap off metal chips that catch on its cutting edges.

If the taper tap becomes difficult to turn, back it out and change to a plug tap. Be sure to lubricate the hole and the end of the new tap before placing it in the hole. When the hole is threaded, back out the tap carefully so that you will not damage the threads with the cut chips.

For a blind hole *(inset)*, finish the threading with a bottoming tap. Screw in the tap, following the threads of the taper and plug taps, until it touches the bottom of the hole. Stop turning it immediately, then back it out carefully.

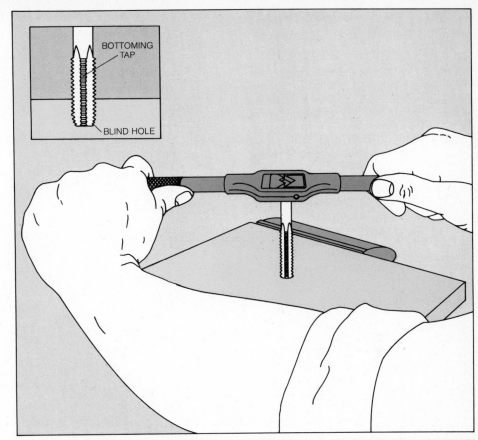

BOTTOMING TAP

BLIND HOLE

4 Cleaning out metal chips. Wearing goggles, gently blow chips out of the threaded hole and off the surface of the workpiece. Clean the hole with cutting fluid squirted on a cotton swab, and clean the workpiece of any remaining metal chips, using a cloth dampened with cutting fluid.

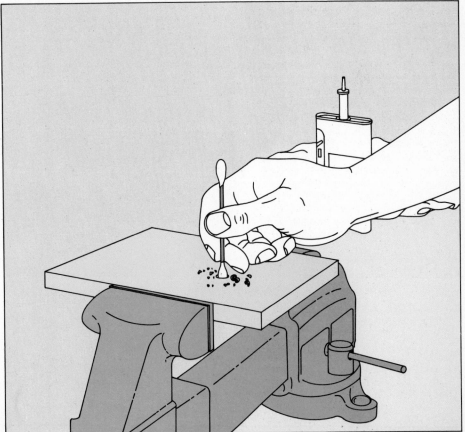

A Drill Press Adapted to Center a Tap

Setting up the drill press. Clamp the metal workpiece to the drill-press table with a C clamp, placing the predrilled hole directly beneath the center of the drill's chuck. Put a dead center—a metal rod with a pointed tip—into the drill chuck. Insert a taper tap in the chuck of a T-handle tap wrench and place it in the hole. Lower the chuck until the dead center is centered over the indentation in the top of the tap, repositioning the workpiece if necessary. There is no need to check the tap for alignment, since the drill press aligns it automatically. Grasp the wrench handle and turn it clockwise to thread the hole. Once the tap is started, raise the drill-press chuck, remove the dead center and finish threading the hole by hand as on pages 30-31.

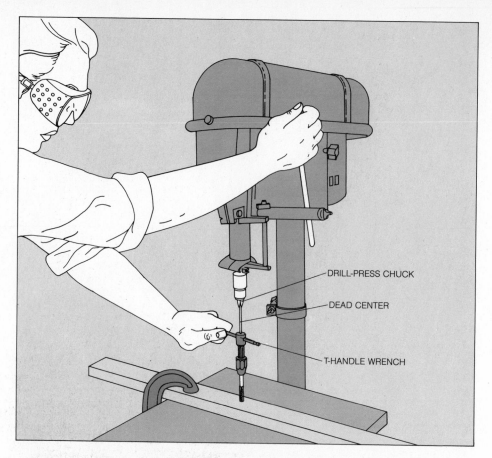

DRILL-PRESS CHUCK

DEAD CENTER

T-HANDLE WRENCH

Threading a Rod with a Die

1 **Adjusting the diestock guide.** Loosen the two guide screws on the base of the diestock that hold the chuck plate and guide fingers in place. Turn the chuck plate clockwise to open the fingers. Slip the diestock, chuck plate up, over the rod, which has been clamped in a vise. Swivel the chuck plate counterclockwise until the guide fingers touch the rod. Open the fingers slightly, just enough to slip the diestock off the rod. Then tighten the two guide screws again, to hold the guide fingers in place.

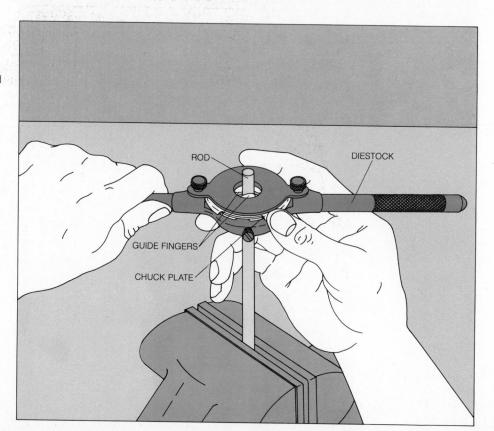

ROD

DIESTOCK

GUIDE FINGERS

CHUCK PLATE

2 **Inserting the die in the diestock.** Hold the diestock, chuck plate down, and loosen the die screw on the side of the diestock. Insert the die in the depression designed to receive it, placing the tapered end of the die's cutting threads face down, against the guide fingers. Then tighten the die screw.

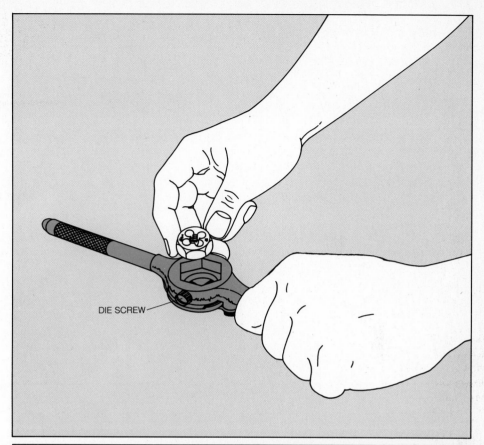

DIE SCREW

3 **Beveling the end of the rod.** To allow the die to grasp the rod tightly, file the bevel around the edge of the rod, using a 10-inch half-round medium-coarse file. Grasp the file at either end and, holding it at about a 30° angle, draw it across the edge of the rod, keeping this angle as nearly as possible around the entire edge.

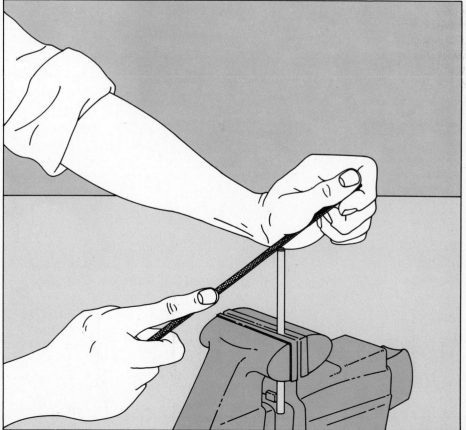

4 **Starting the threads.** Scratch a mark on the rod at the point where you want the threads to end—the depth of the hole into which the rod will fit. Clamp the rod in a vise and place the diestock and die over it, lining up the bottom of the guide with the top of the rod. Turn the chuck plate until the fingers grip the rod tightly; then tighten the screws. Grasp the diestock handles near the die, press down firmly and turn the diestock clockwise to start the threads.

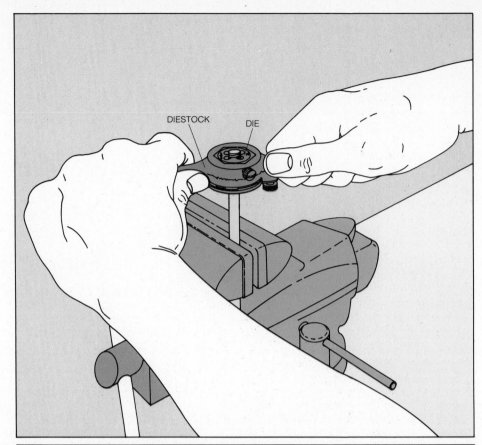

5 **Finishing the threads.** Move your hands to each edge of the diestock and continue threading the rod with a steady motion, backing up a quarter turn to half turn every two full turns, to snap off metal chips. When the guide reaches the mark showing the desired end of the threads, back the die slowly off the rod. Turn the diestock over, put it back on the rod and cut the remaining threads to reach the scratch mark. Clean away any metal chips.

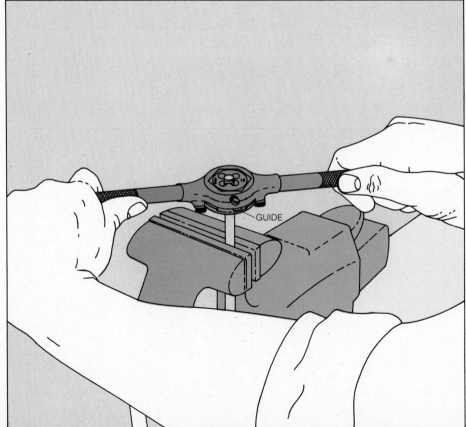

Factory-made Fasteners

When metal parts are made for disassembly or are too thick to be pop-riveted *(page 57)*, the standard way to fasten them is with bolts or screws in threaded holes. These threaded fasteners come in a variety of metals—steel, brass and aluminum—and some have special finishes, such as oxide coating, to prevent corrosion. They are sized by diameter and length, and the length does not include the head—except in the case of oval- and flat-headed machine screws. Threaded fasteners are also graded according to the strength of the metal from which they are manufactured.

The distinctions between bolts and screws intended for use with metal are not as clear-cut as those for wood. Machine screws, for instance, have blunt tips, and stove bolts have slotted heads. But generally bolts are used for heavier work and where the work is accessible from both sides; they are used with nuts. Screws are intended for lighter work that is accessible from only one side. They can be used with or without nuts—except that the hexagonal-headed cap screw is always used with a nut.

In attaching bolts and screws, use the correct tool. Bolts and nuts should be tightened with wrenches, not pliers. Screws and slot-headed stove bolts should be tightened with screwdrivers whose tips fit snugly into the head slots.

Metalworking screws. Machine screws have four different head styles—oval, fillister, round and flat. The common sizes are No. 8 through No. 14; these range in diameter from 3/16 to 5/16 inch and from 1/2 to 4 inches long. The hexagonal nuts sometimes used with them are like those for bolts but are smaller; square nuts are also used. Cap screws are threaded only partway along the shank and are used to join two parts where only one part has a tapped, threaded hole. They range from 1/4 to 1 1/2 inches in diameter and from 1/2 to 6 inches in length. Thumbscrews, used when parts need to be taken apart, come in the same sizes and widths as machine screws and have either a flat or a winged head. Lag screws, also called lag bolts, have a bolt-type head but are threaded like a screw and are used to attach metal to wood. They are available in the same sizes as carriage bolts.

Metalworking bolts, washers and nuts. Machine bolts, used in heavy-duty assembly, have either hexagonal or square heads; common sizes include diameters from 1/4 to 1/2 inch and lengths from 1 to 6 inches. They are used to join two pieces of metal, only one of which is threaded. Tap bolts are similar to machine bolts and come in the same sizes, but they are threaded along the entire body; they are used to fasten two threaded pieces of metal, achieving a close fit. Stove bolts, smaller than machine or tap bolts, have round or flat heads and are commonly available in diameters from 1/8 to 5/16 inch and lengths from 3/8 to 3 inches. They are used mostly in stoves and are tightened and loosened with a screwdriver. Stud bolts are used to fasten two parts together when you may wish to remove one part without removing the bolt from the other part; they have an unthreaded center and come in the same size as machine bolts. Carriage bolts, used for joining metal to wood, have round heads with square collars at the top of the shank and are available in the same sizes as machine bolts.

Common bolt nuts are hexagonal so they can be tightened with a wrench. A cap nut covers the bolt end. Wing nuts are for parts that are disassembled frequently. The thin nut called a jam nut is often used as a washer, to lock a bolt and nut in place; it may also be used alone for a tight but adjustable fit. Nuts come in the same diameters as bolts. The two common types of washers, the flat washer and the lock washer, also come in standard sizes; lock washers are made to press against the work and the nut.

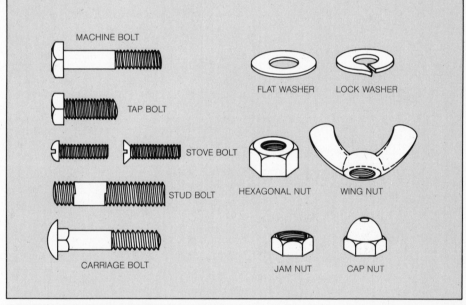

MACHINE BOLT

TAP BOLT

STOVE BOLT

STUD BOLT

CARRIAGE BOLT

FLAT WASHER   LOCK WASHER

HEXAGONAL NUT   WING NUT

JAM NUT   CAP NUT

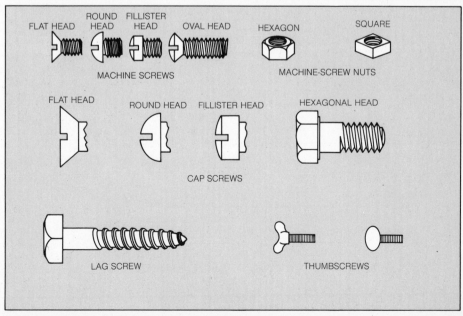

FLAT HEAD   ROUND HEAD   FILLISTER HEAD   OVAL HEAD   HEXAGON   SQUARE

MACHINE SCREWS   MACHINE-SCREW NUTS

FLAT HEAD   ROUND HEAD   FILLISTER HEAD   HEXAGONAL HEAD

CAP SCREWS

LAG SCREW   THUMBSCREWS

2 Strong Sheets Easy to Shape

Rolled into a thin sheet, metal still retains great strength. Even at a thickness more conveniently expressed in a gauge number than as a tiny fraction of an inch, sheet metal has remarkable durability: The sheet-steel skin of a modern metal roof, typically less than $1/60$ inch thick, will cope with wind, rain, hail and snow for 25 years or more. Yet such a sheet is easy to cut and shape. The language of sheet-metal work is revealing: Sheet is shaped with a paper pattern, cut with snips or shears, edged with hems, and joined with seams. The very terms suggest the easy workability of paper or cloth; gone are the files, wrenches and heavy hammers necessary for work with other kinds of cold metal.

Because sheet is so easy to cut, fold and bend, sheet-metal work does not demand much technical cunning. Instead, its challenge lies in what is called pattern development: The ability to visualize a finished, three-dimensional article—a tub or a range hood or a flaring section of duct—unfastened, unfolded, and flattened out in two dimensions, so that an appropriate shape can be drawn on a flat piece of sheet-metal stock.

Galvanized steel—steel that is clad with a thin coat of zinc to protect it from rust—is the modern staple of this venerable craft, which has filled essential needs ever since the days when households depended on coppersmiths or tinmen for their pots, kettles and lanterns. As the stuff of which corrugated "tin" roofs, buckets and heating ducts are made, galvanized sheet may seem a prosaic material. But its origin in the furnaces and rolling mills of giant steel plants involves a complex and dramatic process.

Following the fiery process by which iron is purified and alloyed with precise quantities of carbon to make steel, the liquid metal is cooled slightly and solidifies. Slabs of steel, typically weighing 10 tons, pass through a series of rollers while still at white heat. At that temperature (2,200° to 2,400° F.), the steel is plastic enough to withstand repeated kneading and squeezing, which eventually reduces it to as little as $1/16$ inch in thickness. Pickling the hot-rolled sheet in an acid bath to clean it and cold-rolling it under enormous pressure yield thinner, harder sheets—down to $1/80$ inch. Such very thin sheets are most often used in residential construction and household fittings.

To ready it for zinc coating, the cold-rolled sheet is alternately bathed in hot acid and cold water three or four times. Thoroughly clean after this regimen, the steel is heated to match the temperature of a vat of molten zinc, then dipped. As the zinc film cools, its crystalline structure crazes the shiny surface into spangled confusion—the typical finish on a galvanized sheet.

First Steps in Working a Versatile Material

Light sheet metal—metal rolled thin enough to be shaped with hand tools—is one of the most versatile materials for home-improvement projects. It sheathes the roofs and sides of buildings, and it forms gutters and flashing, ductwork and exhaust hoods. It can be rolled into cylinders, folded into boxes and, depending on the kind of metal, used for objects that are both decorative and practical.

Sheet metals of stainless steel and copper are prized for their luster, aluminum for its light weight and resistance to rust, and galvanized steel—steel with a coating of zinc to forestall rust—for its low cost and easy handling properties. Galvanized steel is the metal of choice for most household projects.

All sheet metals come in a range of thicknesses up to ¼ inch—the point at which sheet metal becomes known as plate. But the measuring systems for thicknesses vary. Measurements of stainless and galvanized steel are expressed either in decimal parts of an inch or in gauge numbers. The gauge is based on the United States Standard system for iron and steel sheet. The lower the gauge number, the greater the thickness.

The thickness of aluminum sheet is also indicated by measurements in decimal parts of an inch; copper is generally classed by weight, in ounces per square foot. For example, 16-ounce copper (.02 inch thick) is used for flashing on commercial roofing; 24-ounce (.032 inch) for decorative items, such as exhaust hoods.

Nonferrous metals (those with little or no iron content) may also be sized by gauge numbers; these gauges are based on a second system, known as Brown & Sharpe or American Standard. In this system the precise thickness of each gauge is slightly different from that of gauge numbers of the United States Standard system, a difference to keep in mind when you are buying sheet metal.

For most household projects, such as rectangular or round ductwork, containers and plant boxes, the most commonly used gauges of galvanized-steel sheet are 30 and 28 (.0125 and .0157 of an inch). Metal in these sizes is flexible enough to handle easily but rigid enough to ensure a sturdy product. Occasionally you may need a stiffer sheet, 26 gauge, for projects such as a toolbox or an exhaust hood. And if you are replacing a section of duct, you will need to match the gauge of the existing metal. A gauge guide (below) simplifies this measurement.

Whatever the gauge, most sheet metal comes 2 to 4 feet wide and 8 to 10 feet long. Because large sheets are difficult to handle, it is advisable to have the metal rolled or cut into manageable sections before you carry it home. To estimate the size of these sections, you will need to make a paper or cardboard pattern of the sheet-metal object, unfolded and flattened out. Called a stretch-out, this pattern will also be your cutting guide. It should contain precise measurements for all the critical dimensions of the finished object, plus tabs of extra material for seams and for the rolled and folded hems that blunt the sharp edges of the sheet metal and make them stronger.

With the stretch-out completed, you can transfer the pattern to the metal by pricking and scoring it; then you can cut and bend the metal and fasten it, much as if you were working with paper. In one important way, however, cutting sheet metal differs from cutting paper: It can be dangerous. Each cut you make exposes sharp edges and creates burrs that can cut a finger.

Never run your hands over a cut edge, and always file down burrs promptly. Keep your work surface free of scrap; metal waste also has hazardous edges. Handle metal sheets with care, especially if they are wet; moisture mixed with oil and dirt can slick the surface and make it hard to grasp. Finally, make sure your hammers are solid and your shears are sharp, wear gloves whenever possible and always wear goggles.

A Gauge to Measure Very Thin Sheets

A circular guide to sheet-metal sizes. Metal sheets and plates can be measured in the slots of this circular gauge. To check metal thickness, file any burrs from the edge being measured, then find the slot into which the edge fits snugly and read the corresponding gauge number embossed above the slot. On the reverse side, the gauge gives an alternate reading of sheet thickness in thousandths of an inch.

The gauge shown carries the United States Standard gauge numbers for sizing iron and steel. A similar gauge, which has slightly different slot widths and numerical designations, measures the standard sizes of aluminum, brass, copper and other nonferrous metals. (Both systems are also used in Canada.)

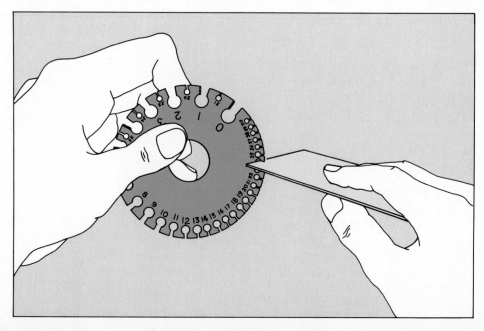

Designs for Safe Edges and Secure Joints

Three hem styles. A simple folded hem, also called a safe edge, requires only a single fold in the metal edge. Allow an extra ½ inch of metal for the folded portion as you draw your paper pattern. A double hem, folded twice, creates a stronger finished edge. For a ¼-inch double hem, again leave an extra ½ inch of metal, but add a bit extra to allow for the thickness of the doubled metal created by the first fold.

Rolling the edge over rust-resistant copper or galvanized-steel wire of about 12 gauge creates a wired edge, the strongest of these three hem styles. It is especially suitable for buckets and tubs, where a rim that resists denting and crumpling is desirable. For this edge add extra material to your pattern amounting to 2½ times the diameter of the wire, plus twice the thickness of the metal itself.

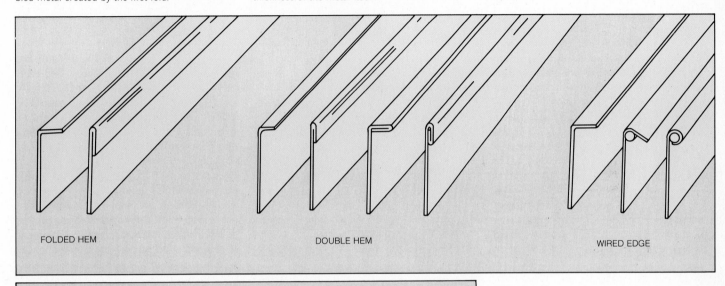

FOLDED HEM   DOUBLE HEM   WIRED EDGE

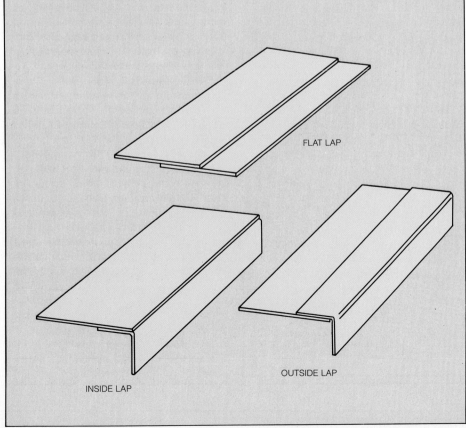

FLAT LAP

INSIDE LAP   OUTSIDE LAP

Lap seams. In this simplest sheet-metal joint, shown flat and in two corner versions, the two edges to be secured are simply laid one over the other. They are then riveted, screwed or soldered together *(pages 56 and 60)*. Often used to seal rectangular ducts and small cylinders and for the vertical seams in boxes, lap seams require an allowance of ½ to 1 inch of extra metal. Despite their simplicity, lap seams can be made watertight with a thin band of solder placed along the inside of the seam *(page 60)*.

Lock seams. These folded joints yield strong seams that will hold with or without the extra bonding of rivets, solder or screws. For standing and folded seams, the edges are folded before joining, then hooked together. A grooved seam is also prefolded, but after the edges are hooked together, one side is hammered down to produce a flush surface. A double seam, used at corners, also requires an initial fold on both edges, then a second fold after the edges are hooked together.

Each type of lock seam has its characteristic applications. Standing seams are often used in assembling large heating and air-conditioning ducts; folded seams link sheets of metal roofing; grooved seams link flat sheets and form lengthwise joints on cylinders, such as sheet-metal pipes, and on rectangular ducts. Double seams most often attach the bases of round or rectangular containers such as buckets or deep boxes. A thin band of solder along the inside of a lock seam will make it watertight.

The extra material needed for each of these seams depends on the size of the seam, the number of folds it involves and the thickness of the metal. A 1-inch standing seam, typical on a large duct, will need ⅞ inch extra metal for the edge with the single fold, 1⅞ inches extra for the edge with the double fold, plus a bit extra for the thickness of the metal.

When you are planning for folded or grooved seams, both of which are typically ¼ inch wide, allow for ¼-inch folds on each edge, plus a small additional amount to accommodate the thickness of the folds. When a folded seam or a grooved seam is used to join the lengthwise edges of a duct or a pipe, be sure that you enlarge the pattern by the width of the seam—in this case ¼ inch—to allow for the reduction in circumference caused by the seam. A standard ¼-inch double seam requires a ¼-inch allowance along the wall of the container where the wall will be joined to the base and ½ inch of extra metal to accommodate the two folds along the edge of the base, along with small additional allowances for the thickness of the folds.

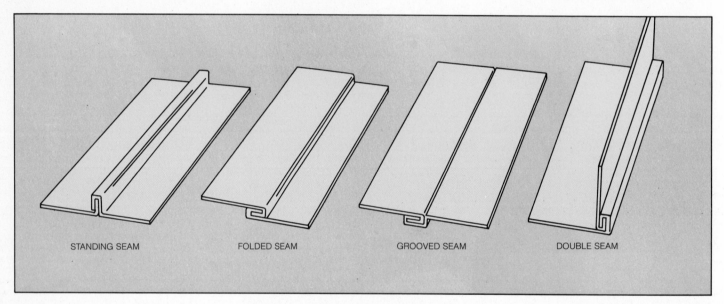

STANDING SEAM   FOLDED SEAM   GROOVED SEAM   DOUBLE SEAM

Drafting Paper Patterns for Simple Shapes

A stretch-out for a rectangular duct. Rule off two parallel lines on a strip of cardboard or stiff paper, making the distance between the lines equal to the desired length of the finished duct. Mark off the lines into four panels, alternating in size, making the first and third panels the size of the duct sides, the second and fourth panels the size of the duct top and bottom. Mark the fold lines between panels with *Xs*. Make a 60° notch about ⅝ inch deep at each end of the fold lines, and angle the four corners of the stretch-out. For a simple lap seam, add a tab of the desired width at one end of the stretch-out. Cut out the stretch-out, and fold it to make sure the duct will be the proper size *(inset)*.

To fasten duct sections together, slide the adjacent edges into slotted sheet-metal strips called S slips, then screw or rivet the joints tight.

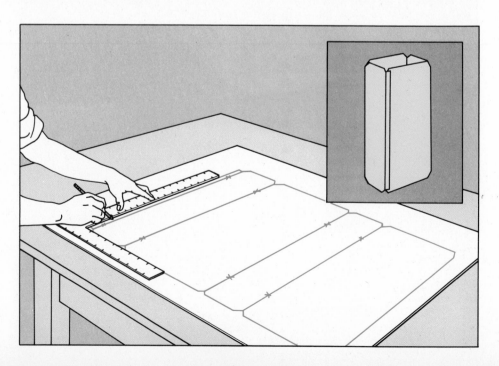

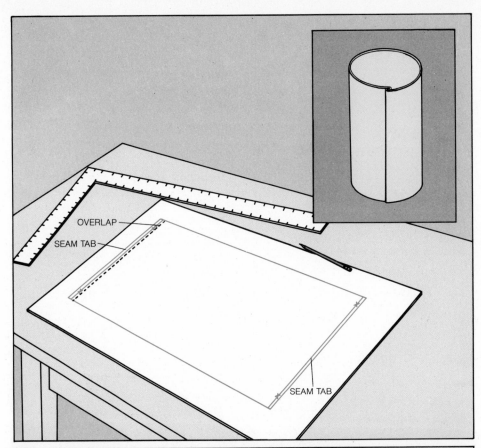

Fashioning a cylinder. Using a ruler and a steel square, draw a stretch-out equal in length to the circumference of the completed cylinder, with an extra allowance of ¼ inch for the overlap in a folded seam; to calculate the circumference, multiply the desired diameter by 3.14. Make the width of the stretch-out equal to the length of the completed cylinder. For the folded seam add two ¼-inch tabs, one at each end. Mark the fold lines with *Xs* to distinguish them from the body of the pattern. Cut out the stretch-out, and roll it to check its dimensions.

OVERLAP

SEAM TAB

SEAM TAB

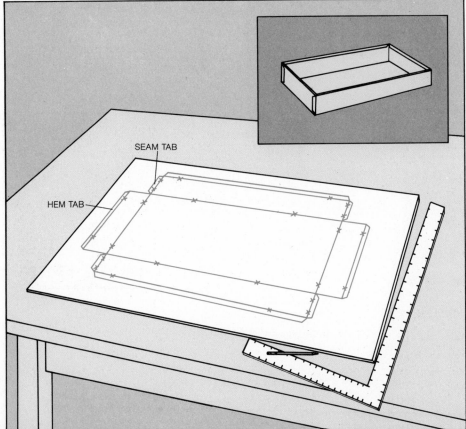

Plotting a basic box. Begin the stretch-out with a rectangle whose dimensions equal those of the bottom of the planned box. Extend the rectangle to form the box sides, making these extensions equal in width to the planned height of the box. Add two tabs for lap seams to the ends of two opposite sides, four tabs in all; then add the desired hem allowance to the outer edge of all four sides. Angle the ends of the hem and seam allowances for a neater finish. Mark all the fold lines with *Xs*. Cut out the pattern, and assemble the box to check it for size and shape.

SEAM TAB

HEM TAB

Transferring a Paper Pattern to Sheet Metal

1 **Pricking the reference points.** Position the pattern on the metal sheet to produce as little waste as possible, and secure the pattern with masking tape. Using a ball-peen hammer and a prick punch, mark the metal at each corner of the bottom and sides and at the corners of the hem and seam tabs. At each *X* that marks a fold line, tap lightly through the pattern to the metal, just barely marking the metal.

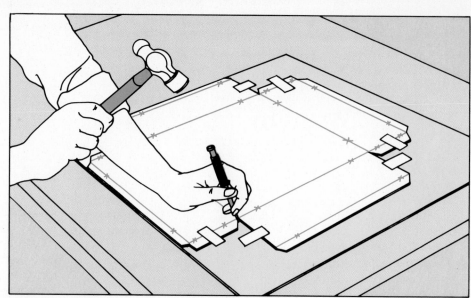

2 **Scribing the outline.** Line up the edge of a steel ruler flush with the edge of the pattern and, using a scriber, lightly scratch the outline of the pattern onto the metal. Keep the point of the scriber pressed firmly against the ruler edge, so that the outline is true. Then lift the pattern off the metal and set it aside.

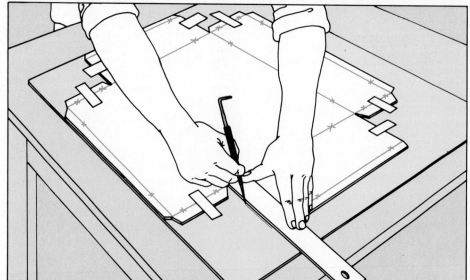

3 **Marking the fold lines.** With the scriber and the steel ruler, retrace the faint outline you have just scratched around the outside of the pattern. Then line up the ruler with the prick marks indicating corners and fold lines, and lightly scribe the fold lines. Be careful not to scribe these lines too deeply, lest you weaken the seams, hems and corner folds. When all of the lines on the paper pattern are visible on the metal, you are ready to begin cutting.

Cutting Out a Flat Metal Shape

Cutting sheet metal to the needed shape and size is the intermediate step in fashioning any sheet-metal object—the step between laying out the pattern *(page 38)* and bending and fastening the metal into its final form *(page 48)*. Because of its relative thinness and flexibility, sheet metal up to 22-gauge can be cut with hand tools almost as effortlessly as paper is cut with scissors. Thicker sheet metal should, like metal plate, be cut with a hacksaw *(page 13)*.

Aviation snips are the most common tools for cutting both straight and curved lines; they are available at any hardware store. Variations on the basic aviation-snip design, useful for special jobs, are also available. For example, hawk-billed snips are best for cutting tight, inside curves; double-cutting shears, with three blades, are made specifically for cutting around cylinders.

Another way to cut through sheet metal is with a punch. For hole punching, a backing material is important—to keep the punch from cutting into the work surface below and to avoid distorting the hole in the metal. A block of soft lead or the end grain of a wood block is best for this purpose. Do not use the side of a wood block; it is softer than the end, and the punch will depress the wood, resulting in a jagged, irregular hole.

Both snips and punches require maintenance. Sharp, nick-free blades are a must for snips; sharpening is done with a specially designed file and can be tricky because the snip's blades are beveled, so this job is best left in the hands of a professional. Punches, too, should be sharpened periodically.

Keep the joints of your snips well adjusted by tightening the pivot bolt that holds the sides of the tool together. To keep the snips working smoothly, oil this joint occasionally with household oil or a silicone lubricant.

A few power tools work well as sheet-metal cutters. For cutting holes of various sizes, you can use a hand-held electric drill or a drill press fitted with special bits for sheet metal. For cutting large patterns that have either straight or curved lines, you can use a hand-held power shear or a band saw.

If you choose to work with a band saw,

use the right blade for the job. The least expensive and most practical blades for the home workshop are high-carbon steel blades with hardened teeth and a soft, flexible back. Blades ranging in width from 3/32 inch to 1 inch are available; the narrower the blade, the smaller the radius it will cut. The number of teeth per inch is another factor in blade selection. A blade with 10 or fewer teeth per inch should be used for soft, thick metals. A blade with 12 or more teeth per inch does a better job of cutting hard, thin metal pieces. When you buy a metal-cutting blade, ask the dealer about the speed at which it should be used.

Before using a band saw to cut metal, be sure its parts are adjusted correctly. First adjust the blade tension according to the saw manufacturer's instructions. The blade guides, which flank the blade on either side, should be tightened directly against the blade, then loosened until a piece of paper can be slipped between each guide and the blade.

As with all metalworking, safety rules must be followed to avoid injury. Always wear gloves and goggles, and file all edges as soon as possible after cutting.

Hand tools for cutting sheet metal. These hand-held snips, shears and punches are used for cutting sheet metal to any shape or size. Aviation snips—there are three standard types—have serrated blades that are curved and beveled to make a specific kind of cut: a straight line, as shown here, a right-hand curve or a left-hand curve. Widely available brands have color-coded grips for quick identification in the workshop.

Hawk-billed snips have long handles and slender blades, making them especially useful for cutting curves in tight spots. Also handy for short, hard-to-reach inside cuts is the ripping shear. Punches, when tapped repeatedly with a ball-peen hammer, make holes of various sizes. The solid punch pushes small circular sections out of a metal sheet; the hollow punch works like a cookie cutter to remove larger circular sections. A hand-held power shear makes quick work of big jobs; its reciprocating blade shears easily along both straight and curved guidelines.

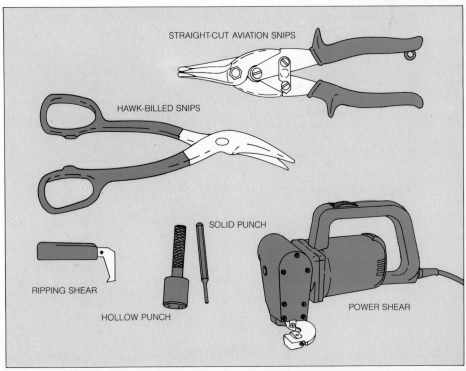

STRAIGHT-CUT AVIATION SNIPS

HAWK-BILLED SNIPS

SOLID PUNCH

RIPPING SHEAR

HOLLOW PUNCH

POWER SHEAR

Aviation Shears for Straight Lines and Curves

Cutting a straight line. Select snips designed for straight cutting. Set the work on a flat surface, grasp the metal with one hand and insert the metal between the blades, at the guideline, pushing the snips forward as far as they will go. Keeping the snip grips perpendicular to the metal surface, squeeze firmly until the blades close to within ¼ inch of their tips. Do not close the blades completely—this will cause burrs and irregularities along the cut edge. Open the blades slowly while applying gentle forward pressure in the direction of the cut, then close them again in the same manner, repeating this action until the cut is completed. Push the waste metal away from you in an upward or downward curve to avoid cutting your gloves. When the cut is done, file the edge *(page 16)* to remove any burrs.

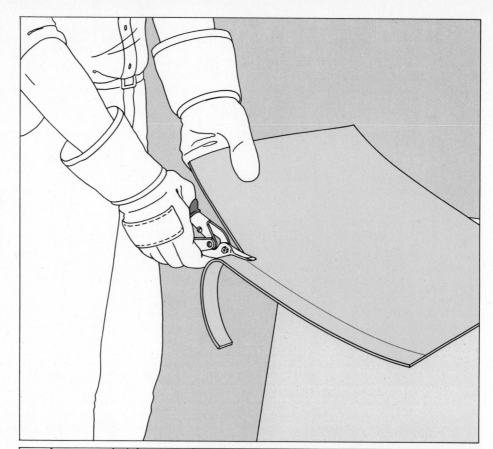

Cutting along a broad curve. Using snips designed for curve cutting, begin as for a straight cut, with the metal held flat and the guideline pushed as far between the snip blades as it will go. Continue the cut, keeping the grips perpendicular to the metal surface; but angle them slightly to the right or left to follow the guideline. The blades, because of their shape, will automatically cut along the curve; do not force them. Push waste metal away from you, and file the cut edge to remove burrs.

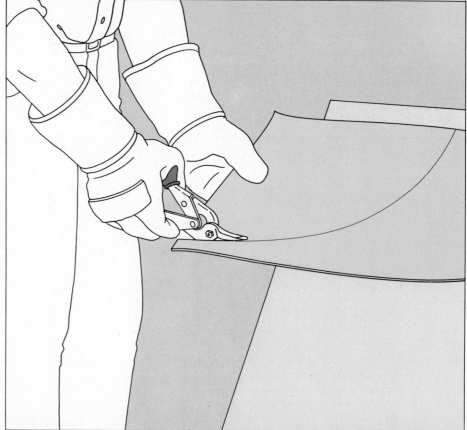

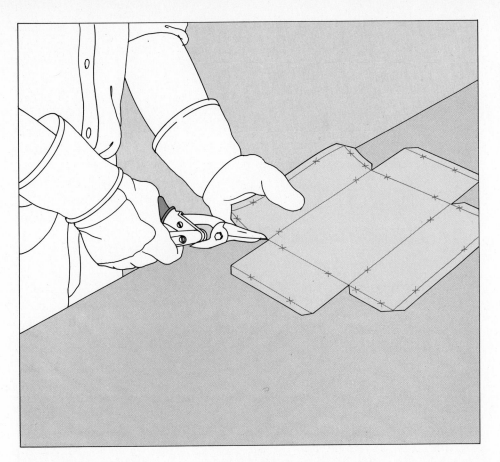

Snipping a notch in a cutout. Use straight-cut aviation snips to make the notches in a sheet-metal cutout *(page 40, bottom)*. Hold the blades over the notch guideline, aligning the tips with the point of the notch. Cut, closing the blade tips completely at the corner of the notch.

Cutting a Large Hole with Punch and Snips

1 Beginning the cut with a punch. Set the approximate center of the projected hole over the end-grain portion of a hardwood block or over a soft lead block. Set the head of a hollow punch within the scribed guideline and over the block, press down firmly and, with the flat poll of a ball-peen hammer, strike a solid blow on the shank of the punch. Try to punch entirely through the metal with no more than two blows—repeated light taps will result in a jagged edge.

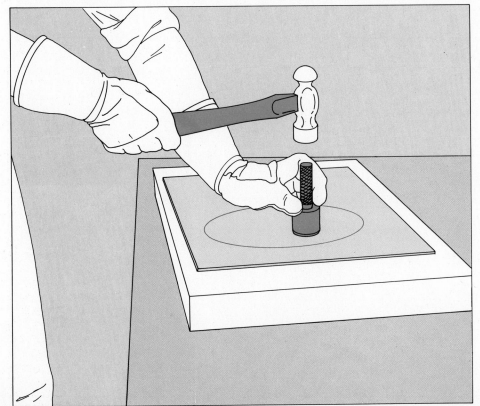

2 **Cutting with hawk-billed snips.** Working from above or below the metal surface, whichever is more comfortable, cut in an arc-shaped path from the edge of the punched hole to within ¼ inch of the scribed guideline, using the technique described for aviation snips *(page 44)*. Continue cutting just inside the guideline, periodically bending the waste metal away from your hand. When the cut is completed, discard the waste, then go back and cut directly along the guideline, trimming the hole to size.

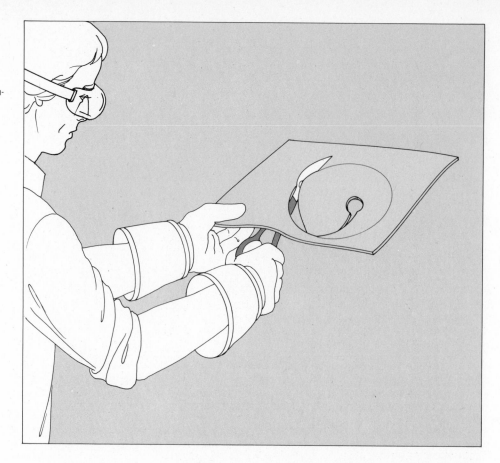

A Ripping Shear to Make Small Inside Cuts

Cutting with a ripping shear. Set the pointed tip of the shear at the midpoint of a scribed guideline. Tap the head of the shear lightly with the flat poll of a ball-peen hammer to drive the point through the metal; then, with repeated light taps, drive the shear blade along the guideline. Complete corners in a pattern by cutting toward them from opposite directions, rather than by cutting around them in one direction.

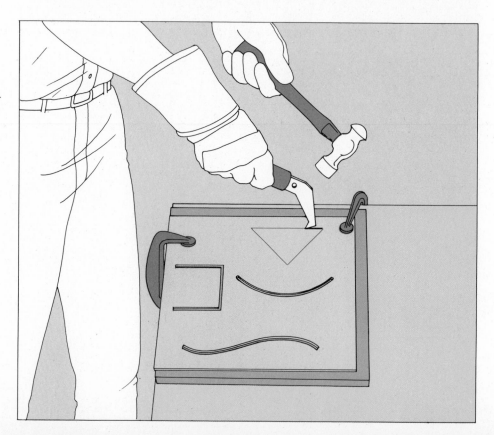

Two Power Tools for Faster Metal Cutting

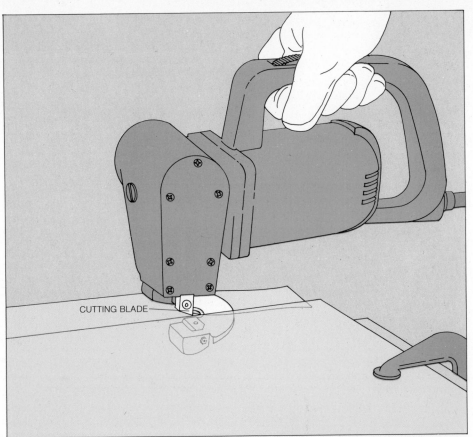

CUTTING BLADE

Cutting with a hand-held power shear. Clamp or hold the metal to be cut so that the guideline overhangs the edge of the work surface, then set the shear blade against the edge of the metal and turn on the power. Push the blade firmly and steadily along the guideline, but do not force the shear forward faster than the blade can cut. Stop periodically to bend waste metal away, and file the edge when the cut is finished.

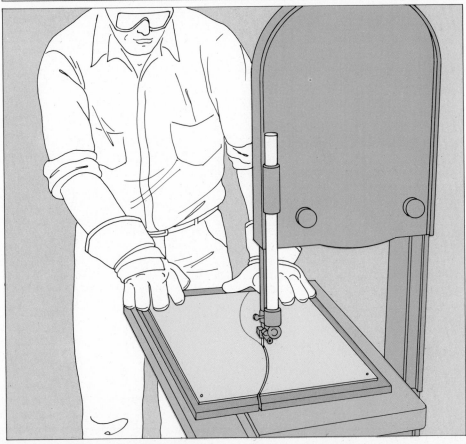

Cutting sheet metal with a band saw. Set the blade guides so that they are no more than ¼ inch above the surface of the metal to be cut; position the metal, tacked to a plywood backing, on the saw table, aligning the blade with the beginning of the guideline. Turn on the saw, and push the metal and plywood forward into the blade with one hand, directing them with the other so that the blade cuts slightly to the waste side of the guideline. Apply steady, constant pressure, pushing only as fast as the blade will easily cut. When the cut is completed, file the metal edge to remove any burrs.

Folds and Bends for Three-dimensional Shapes

Two basic operations—folding and bending—transform a flat sheet-metal cutout *(page 43)* into a completely shaped article ready for fastening with rivets, screws or solder. In commercial shops, the curves of cylinders and the sharply folded corners of boxes are made largely by machine; but you can duplicate many forms by hand, using sheet metal of 24-gauge or lighter, to make ducts, gutters, flashing, boxes and buckets.

Many of the tools you will need are much the same as those used by tinmen of past centuries. For example, a mallet with a wooden or rubber head works better than a steel hammer for coaxing metal into shape, because its softer head will not dent the sheet. To make the edge folds for seams and hems, you will need a hand seamer *(opposite)*, also called hand tongs, available at metal-supply stores. Look for a model equipped with screw stops to limit the capacity of the hinged jaws, ensuring that you grasp the same amount of edge each time you reposition the seamer to extend a fold.

For the final folds and tucks on the wired edges of container rims and the double seams of container bases, the tapered peen of a setting hammer serves best, allowing you to focus your blows on narrow ledges of metal. For finishing joints, special slotted tools called hand groovers and grooving rails squeeze the folded seam into a ridge on one side of the metal and leave the other side flush and smooth.

Traditionally, a set of stakes—steel knobs, spikes, and blades—is considered a necessity in a metal workshop. The stakes stand on hefty shanks that fit into a plate bolted to the workbench, and they serve as forms on which the sheet metal can be shaped by hand or mallet. Each of the many kinds of stakes is designed for a specific fold or bend; the horns of some stakes can also be used to support a formed sheet-metal article as

you close the seams and finish the edges in the final steps of shaping. Available only through metal-supply stores, stakes are expensive individually or as a set, but you can improvise many with sections of pipe or rail clamped between wooden blocks in a bench vise.

Before final shapes can be formed, the hems and seams indicated by the pattern *(pages 39-40)* must be folded to reinforce and bind the cut edges of the flat metal sheet and to make them less hazardous. These folds are formed with a hand seamer while the sheet is still flat. Wired edges for the rims of cylindrical objects should also be finished before the sheet is shaped. On more complex sheet-metal shapes, such as boxes, cones and tapers, the wiring is added after the shaping and seaming are finished. However, in forming a box, the open folds into which the wire will be fitted should be formed on the flat sheet.

For folded and grooved seams, as for hems and edges, use a hand seamer to make open-edged folds, called seam locks, before you shape the flat sheet. Leave clearance under the folds so that the folds will slip together easily on the finished article. And form them on opposite sides of the flat sheet so that they will interlock.

Once the edge folds and seams have been creased, the sharp bends that define the corners of boxes and rectangular forms—and the curved bends that shape cylinders and tapered shapes—are made. For each kind of bend, use the appropriate stake or improvise. You can make an angular bend, for instance, by securing the metal with an angle iron and clamps and creasing it over the edge of the workbench. The sides of a box can be formed with the help of a wooden block, cut to size and clamped to the bottom of the box so that the sides can be bent up against the wood.

A length of pipe clamped firmly in a

vise is an adequate substitute for stakes in shaping curves, cones and tapers. For unusual or complex curves, you can cut wooden formers—interlocking blocks of hardwood—to squeeze the sheet into the shape you want when the two pieces of wood, with metal between them, are clamped in a vise.

With the article bent and folded into its final form, securing the seams is a simple matter of hooking the seam locks, then hammering them flat to form folded seams. In seaming articles with curved sides, a piece of pipe clamped in a vise will again support the operation. For boxes or open-ended rectangles, you can support the piece by attaching a length of flat bar stock or railroad rail to the edge of the bench.

For an even more secure seam, finish the joint with a hand groover. Select a grooving tool with a slot about 1/16 inch wider than the seam itself. If you are forming a number of articles with grooved seams, settle on a common seam size: If you plan for 1/4-inch seams throughout, for example, you can then finish every seam with a standard 5/16-inch (No. 2) hand groover.

Several metal-shaping operations present special problems. Attaching the base of a container to a cylindrical or tapered wall with a double seam, or wiring the rim of a tapered article, requires that you make sharp folds along curved rims and edges. Metal shops use heavy rollers and rotary machines to turn these flanges, but a pair of flat-nosed pliers, the jaws wrapped in masking tape to avoid marring the metal, makes a reasonable substitute. A mallet and a setting hammer are used for crimping the folded metal around a wire to form a wired edge or for locking the flanges together in a double seam. In turning a flange with pliers, as in shaping sheet metal with any hand tool, work slowly and patiently to avoid stretching or kinking the metal.

Hems and Seam Locks Made with Folds

Making a preliminary fold. Using a hand seamer, grasp the middle of the edge that is to be bent, positioning the jaws of the seamer so that they close at the fold line previously scribed on the metal *(page 42)*. Tighten the adjusting screws until they butt against the metal edge. Use the edge of the lower jaw as a fulcrum by pressing down firmly against the work surface while you lift the handles of the seamer to start the bend. On a long edge, it is best to work from the middle of the piece to either side, grasping and bending the metal edge every 3 to 4 inches along the fold line. In order to avoid kinking the metal, bend each section only slightly, then move on to the next, bringing it even with the previous section. Continue folding bit by bit until you have worked the edge to an angle halfway between vertical and completely closed. The edge is now ready for wiring, or for further creasing to form a folded hem or a seam lock.

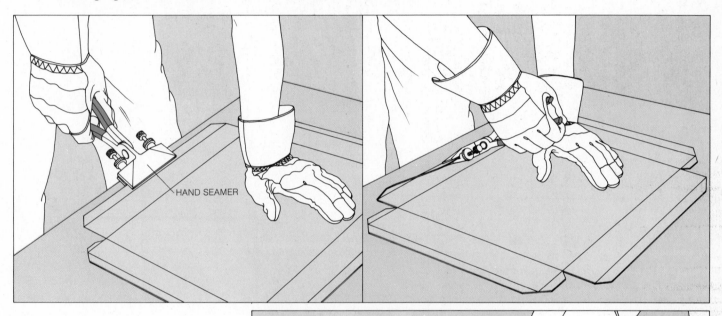

HAND SEAMER

Closing a seam. If you are making a seam lock to join with another in a folded or grooved seam, slip two thicknesses of scrap metal or a thin scrap of wood under the middle of the preliminary fold. Fit the jaws of the seamer over the creased edge and the scrap, and squeeze firmly. Work along the full length of the fold, moving the scrap as you go. Then remove the scrap, and check to make certain that enough clearance remains for the fold to mate with another seam lock.

For a simple folded hem, as on the top edge of a box, leave out the scrap and close the fold completely *(inset)*. For a double hem, fold a single-fold hem a second time, turning the edge with the seamer and crimping it closed.

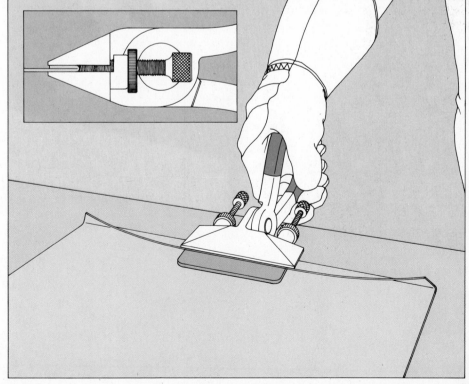

Special Tools Designed to Make Shaping Easier

A gallery of sheet-metal stakes. The rounded end of a hollow mandrel stake supports pipes, buckets and similar articles with curved sides during seaming, grooving and finishing; the squared anvil at the other end provides a surface for seaming and finishing boxes and rectangular ducts. The hatchet stake is used to make angular folds, such as at the corners of a box; its sharp edge creases metal crisply. The two horns of different diameters on the conductor stake shape curves and cylinders of various sizes. Broad cones and tapered objects take shape on the shorter horn of the blowhorn stake; the slender horn is used for shaping longer and narrower cones.

The shanks of the hatchet, conductor, and blowhorn stakes fit into holes on a steel bench plate, made to be bolted to the workbench. Or the stakes can be clamped in a vise. The hollow mandrel stake attaches directly to the bench with a bolt that slides in a groove on the underside of the tool, allowing varying lengths of the stake to extend over the edge of the bench.

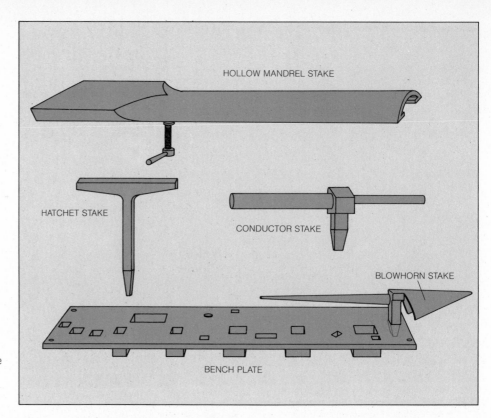

HOLLOW MANDREL STAKE

HATCHET STAKE

CONDUCTOR STAKE

BLOWHORN STAKE

BENCH PLATE

Forming Angles and Simple Curved Objects

Making a right-angled bend. Align the fold line on the metal with the edge of the workbench. Lay an angle iron across the sheet, flush with the fold line and the workbench edge, and clamp it in place with two C clamps. Force the flap of metal down by hand, then square off the bend at a crisp right angle by tapping along the length of the crease with a mallet.

To use a special hatchet stake *(inset)* in forming an angled bend, position the fold line directly over the stake and press down on both sides. When the fold reaches the desired angle, keep the bend fitted tightly over the sharp edge of the stake; pound with a mallet along the crease, to make the bend sharper.

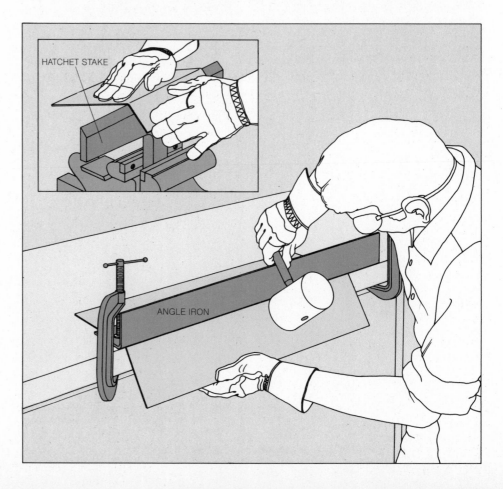

HATCHET STAKE

ANGLE IRON

Bending the sides of a box. Cut a block of wood to the exact width and length of the bottom of the planned box. Center it on the cutout, aligning its edges with the fold lines. Clamp the assembly to the workbench, positioning one fold line directly over and flush with the edge. Bend up the side by hand, and tap along the crease with a mallet to make a sharp bend. Bend up the remaining sides; for each one, unclamp the assembly, turn it, then reposition and reclamp the block so that the next unbent side projects over the workbench edge.

Shaping curves and cylinders. Using a vise, secure a length of pipe with a radius at least 25 per cent smaller than that of the curve or cylinder you plan, or use a conductor stake of the proper size *(inset)*. Support the flat sheet with one edge extending just past the top of the curve, and bend down the sheet in small sections, by hand or with a mallet. Move the sheet gradually across the pipe or stake; a curve formed with widely separated bends will be uneven.

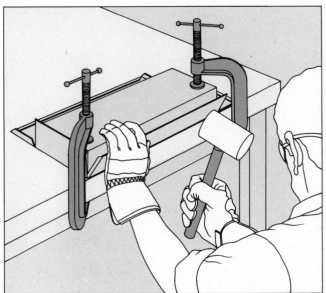

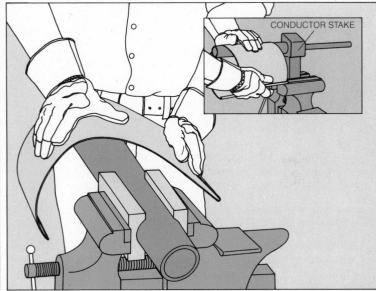

CONDUCTOR STAKE

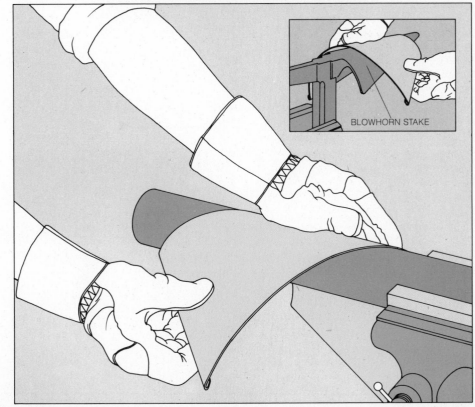

BLOWHORN STAKE

Forming a cone. Starting at one end of the metal cutout, bend the metal down over a piece of pipe clamped in a vise, by hand or with a mallet. Slowly work the narrow end of the cutout across the pipe, bending it sharply where you form the small opening of the cone. Move the wider end of the piece more quickly and bend it less sharply, so that the cone will taper properly.

To shape a cone on a blowhorn stake *(inset)*, form the narrow end of the cone over the point of the horn, the wider end over the broad part of the stake, bending the metal gradually.

Wooden Forming Blocks for Unusual Curves

A pair of hardwood dies. Place the sheet to be bent between two interlocking pieces of a hardwood block, cut to the curved shape you seek. The dies can be cut most easily with a band saw, a jig saw or a saber saw. Fit the assembly between the jaws of a bench vise, and turn the handle until the metal is bent into shape.

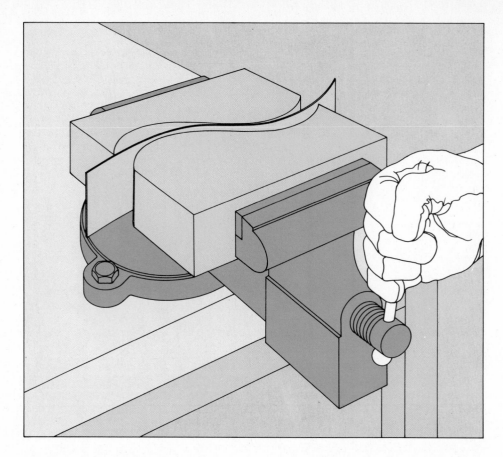

Interlocking Folded Seams

Hooking and hammering. Join the edges of a formed object by hooking the seam locks together. Then support the object on a length of pipe, a piece of rail, or either end of a mandrel stake. Use a rounded surface for a cylindrical form, a flat surface for rectangles and boxes. Turn the object until the seam is directly over the support, then tap along its length with a mallet. Flatten the seam with blows of even pressure, to avoid distorting the metal.

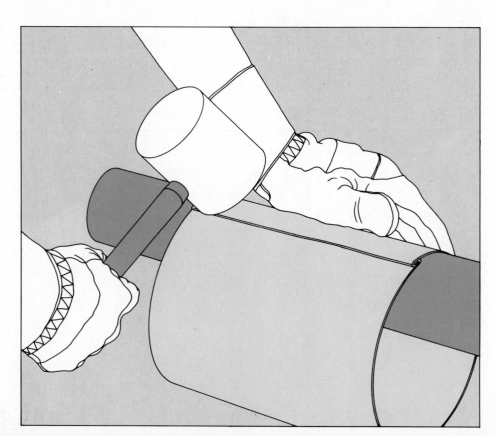

Groovers to Make Seams Flush on One Side

Grooving an outside seam. Support the object, with its seams already joined *(opposite)*, over a stake, pipe or rail. Fit a hand groover of the proper size over one end of the joint, and hammer it sharply to start the groove; repeat at the other end. Tip the groover back down the seam line, and hammer it along the entire length. The three layers of metal in the joint will form a ridge down the outside of the object; the inner surface will stay flush and smooth *(inset)*.

Grooving an inside seam. Clamp a rail with a groove of the proper size to the edge of the bench, rounded face up for cylindrical objects, flat face up for rectangular ducts and boxes. Position the locked seam over the groove, and use a mallet to drive each end of the seam into the groove. Then mallet along the entire length of the joint from end to end, forming a ridge of folded metal on the inside of the piece and a smooth, flush seam on the outside.

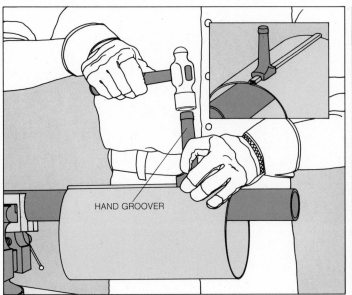

HAND GROOVER

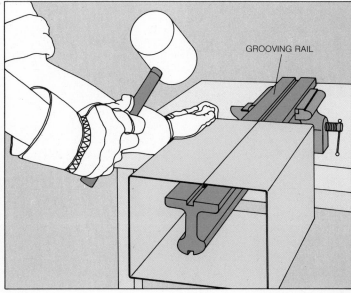

GROOVING RAIL

A Wired Edge for Smooth Reinforcement

1 Bending the wire to fit the rim. Measure and cut a length of wire equal to twice the combined length and width of the box, plus twice the diameter of the wire. Clamp the wire in a vise, with about 1½ inches extending from one side. Hammer that short section to a right-angled bend; then unclamp the wire, and pass through the vise a length equal to one side of the box. Reclamp for a second right-angled bend. Unclamp the wire, and repeat the process twice more. On the fourth side, butt the wire ends together about 1½ inches from the corner bend, not at a corner; this will strengthen the corner seams of the box and give the appearance of continuous wiring around the rim.

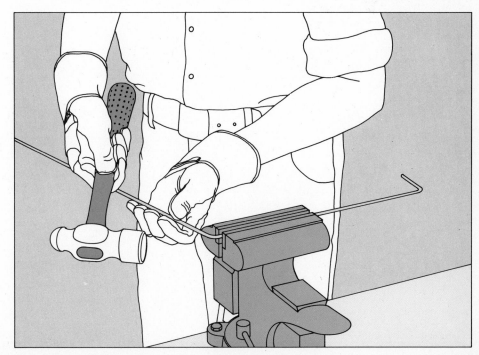

2 Fixing the wire to the rim. Slip the formed wire into the folds left partially open around the top of the box *(page 49)*. Fit the box over an improvised support or the flat end of a mandrel stake; use pliers with taped jaws to press the wire snugly into the fold at one end of a side. Use a mallet to bend the creased edge over the wire. Work along the side in small sections, moving the pliers as you go so that you are always holding the wire close to the section being flattened. Continue all the way around the rim, rotating the box on the support as you work.

3 Setting the edge. Upend the box on the work surface, and crimp the edge farther around the wire by tapping along it with the square face of a setting hammer. To complete the tucking, reverse the hammer and drive the metal edge behind the wire with the hammer's tapered peen.

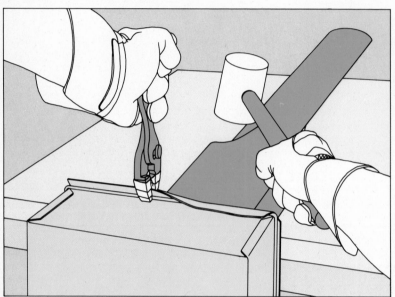

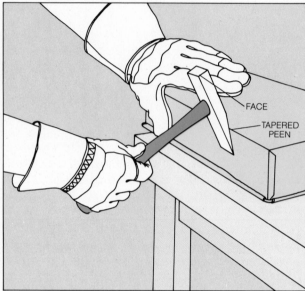

FACE

TAPERED PEEN

Double-seaming around a Container Base

1 Turning the flange. Fit a cylindrical or tapered container wall over a section of pipe or a mandrel stake. Steady your work with one hand and use flat-nosed pliers to grasp the edge marked for folding, bending it up in small sections. Work slowly, and do not bend any section sharply without evening off the rest of the edge.

As the turned-up portion approaches a right angle, remove the container wall from the support. Upend it on the work surface, and strike along the flange with a mallet to square off the bend to form a right angle.

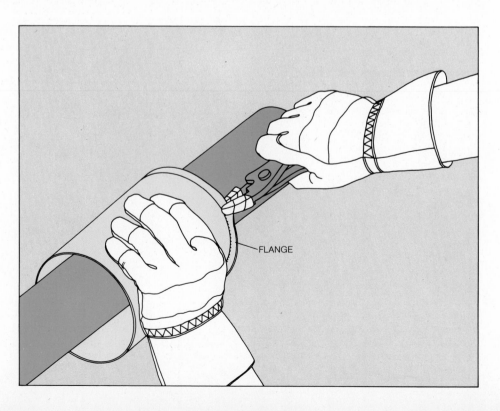

FLANGE

2 **Edging the base.** Form a matching right-angled flange around the container base by bending up the circular edge, marked off with a divider *(page 12)*. Begin by using flat-nosed pliers to crease the edge in small sections around the base. Then position the base against the end of a piece of pipe or a mandrel stake, aligning it so that the folded edge hooks just over the horizontal surface of the pipe or stake. Use a mallet to hammer the edge down onto the curved surface, rotating the base slowly until you finish the flange at a right angle to the base.

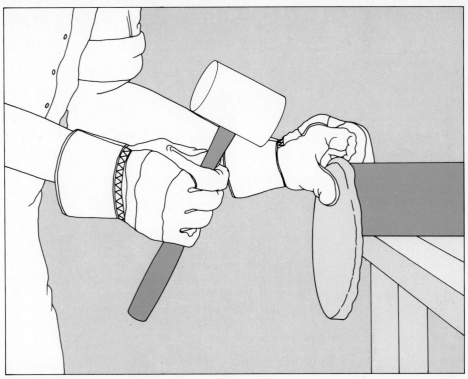

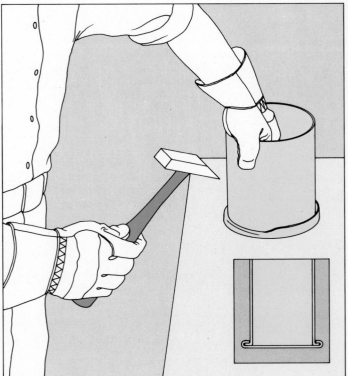

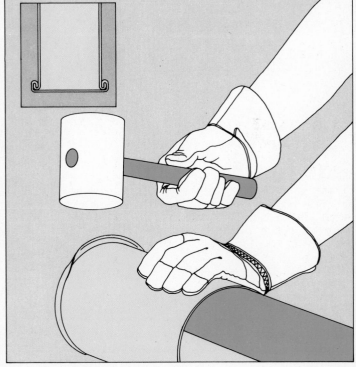

3 **Closing the seam.** With the base flat on a work surface, fit the wall of the container down inside the turned-up flange of the base. Then use the tapered peen of a setting hammer to bend down the edge of the base onto the flange at the bottom of the container wall *(inset)*. Hold the hammer at a sharp angle, so as not to dent or scratch the piece with the hammer head.

4 **Locking the base in place.** Support the container on a pipe or a mandrel stake. Use a mallet to turn up the joined edges of the base and walls so that they lie flat against the container sides *(inset)*, rotating the container as you work around the entire seam.

The Standard Fasteners: Screws or Rivets

Because it is thin, sheet metal must usually be joined with sheet-metal screws or rivets. Sheet-metal screws have sharp, self-tapping threads and strong shafts that resist shearing. And rivets—two-headed fasteners that grip sheet metal from both sides—will not pull out under vibration. Rivets come in two styles, pop rivets and tinner's rivets. Pop rivets are easier to install, but tinner's rivets give a more decorative finish.

Whether you use a sheet-metal screw or a rivet, make sure it is long enough to penetrate the sheet metal completely. Also, choose a fastener of the same metal to make the joint less conspicuous.

A sheet-metal screw cuts its own threads into a drilled or punched hole when the screw tip is placed in the hole, pressed and turned clockwise. It may be installed with a flat-tipped or a Phillips screwdriver or with a nut driver. Sheet-metal screws can be driven by a variable-speed drill or a spiral-ratchet screwdriver equipped with an appropriate bit.

Both tinner's rivets and pop rivets have a shaft that you insert through a drilled hole, with a preformed head at one end of the rivet shaft. But the similarity ends there. With a tinner's rivet, the preformed head is placed on a small steel block and the projecting rivet shaft is held against the top piece of sheet metal with a tool called a rivet set, which is then struck with a ball-peen hammer; the hammered end is finished into a hemispherical head

with either a ball-peen hammer or the rivet set. The tinner's rivet has the disadvantage of requiring access to both sides of the panels that are being joined.

Although it may lack the ornamental appeal of a tinner's rivet, the pop rivet is quickly installed, and you need access to only one side of the joint. The mandrel, a long thin extension from one side of the pop rivet, is mounted in the nosepiece of a pop-rivet tool. The short rivet shaft is inserted in the drilled hole, and the tool pulls the mandrel through the shaft; a ball at the far end of the mandrel compresses the rivet shaft into a rivet head on the other side of the joint. The excess mandrel is snapped off, leaving the rivet securely in place.

Installing Screws to Join Sheet-Metal Parts

Gripping sheet metal with a screw. Punch or drill a hole through both pieces of sheet metal, using a metal-cutting bit of the same diameter as the screw shaft. Place the tip of a sheet-metal screw into the hole, and drive it in with a screwdriver or a nut driver until it is tight.

Installing a screw is speedier if you use a self-drilling sheet-metal screw with a tip shaped like a drill bit *(inset)*. The screw, which drills its own hole, must be turned by a power drill fitted with a screwdriver or nut-driver attachment.

Fastening Joints Using Tinner's Rivets

1 **Setting the rivet.** Drill a hole through the sheet-metal panels and insert the shaft of a tinner's rivet through them. Place the panels over a 3-pound steel block—the bucking bar—with the preformed head of the rivet down. Hold a rivet set over the projecting end of the rivet, with the small hole at the end of the rivet set over the rivet. Rap the rivet set with a ball-peen hammer to form a new head on top of the rivet and seat it against the sheet metal.

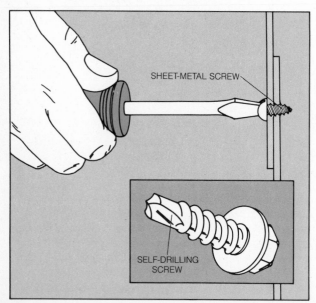

SHEET-METAL SCREW

SELF-DRILLING SCREW

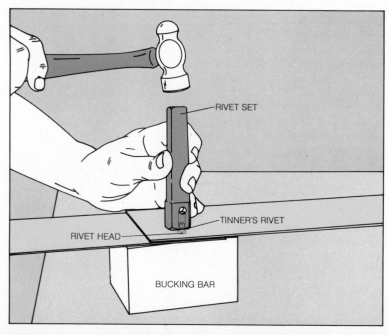

RIVET SET

TINNER'S RIVET

RIVET HEAD

BUCKING BAR

2 **Heading the rivet.** To create a decorative, mottled appearance on the exposed rivet head, beat down on the protruding rivet shaft with the round peen of a ball-peen hammer. Hammer lightly, working in circles around the perimeter of the rivet until it forms a mottled hump, pressed tightly against the sheet-metal panel.

A more uniform rivet head can be formed with the hemispherical indentation on the end of the rivet set *(inset)*. Set the indentation over the rivet shaft, and drive the rivet set straight down with the flat poll of a ball-peen hammer until the rivet set meets the sheet-metal surface.

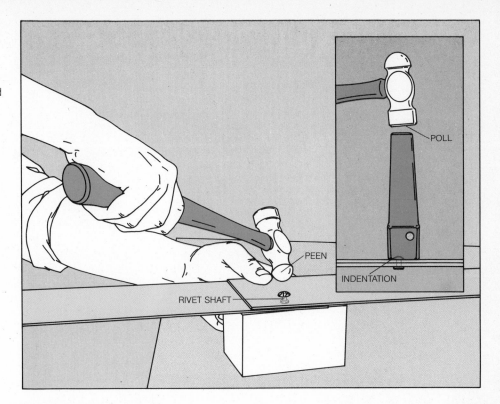

POLL

PEEN

INDENTATION

RIVET SHAFT

Quick Fastening with a Pop-Rivet Tool

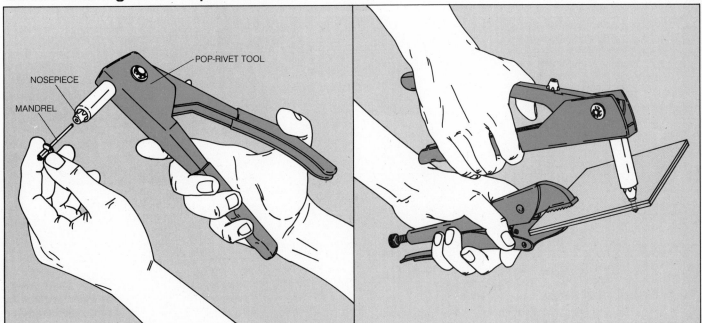

POP-RIVET TOOL

NOSEPIECE

MANDREL

Using a pop-rivet tool. Open the handles of the pop-rivet tool completely and load it by sliding the mandrel of a pop rivet as far as you can into the nosepiece hole *(above, left)*. Squeeze the handles until they grip the mandrel. If possible, firmly grip the sheet-metal parts together; insert the pop rivet into the drilled hole down to the preformed rivet head. Holding the nosepiece of the pop-rivet tool against the sheet metal, alternately open and close the handles of the tool to draw the mandrel up into the nosepiece. The far end of the rivet will be mushroomed by the pull on the mandrel; continue until the handles of the rivet tool no longer move easily. Then squeeze the handles harder to break off the excess mandrel inside the rivet. If the mandrel protrudes, use a small punch and light hammer taps to drive it down.

Temporary strength. Two small blobs of solder, called tacks, hold a pair of metal strips at a right angle to form a T joint. Later the joint will be reheated with an 80-watt soldering iron; solder from the spool, touched to the hot metal, will flow the length of the joint, strengthening it with a continuous bead of metal.

The ancient Greek poet Hesiod, recounting how Prometheus stole fire from the gods and gave it to humans, concluded, "And now, though feeble and short-lived, mankind has flaming fire and therefrom learns many crafts." High among these crafts was metalworking. Fire permitted metal to be smelted from rock and cast into tools and weapons; men thus became the gods of the earth.

Many of the techniques employed in metalworking today still hark back to those used by the first people to beat red-hot bronze into swords or plowshares. Tool-dressers, blacksmiths and farriers (the smiths who shoe horses) still use a coal, coke or wood fire to soften their metal. The casting of molten metal in molds, a modern forming method that is used both industrially and in home workshops to make a variety of metal parts, is rooted in skills first developed more than 6,000 years ago.

As time-tested as some of today's metalworking techniques are, however, others have been profoundly enhanced by modern technology. Welding, for instance, is a painstaking procedure when a blacksmith's forge is used. Entire workpieces must be heated to a temperature that is dangerously close to the ignition point of the metal, and in the process, it is difficult to avoid a deposit of cinders or scale—either of which can fatally weaken the weld. With a modern arc welder, a tool that conveniently harnesses the 7,000°-to-10,000° F. heat of an electric spark, welding can be done with speed and precision that was never imagined by the smiths of yore. Similar precision in welding can be attained with the clean, sharp-pointed flame of an oxyacetylene torch, which may also be equipped with a special tip for bending metal or even with a tip for cutting through a piece of metal with a knife of burning gases.

Metal pieces can also be joined by soldering; unlike welding, soldering relies on man-made alloys that melt at comparatively low temperatures. Somewhat easier to master than welding, soldering is useful where the greater strength of a welded joint is not required—in joining electrical components, for example, or for locking together sheet-metal joints.

Whether the skills one uses to work hot metal are ancient or modern, the emotional concomitants of the work have never changed: the moments of uncertainty before a weld or a casting cools, when the metalworker does not know if the work will be a success; and then—one hopes—the triumph. "This art holds the mind of the artificer in suspense and fear regarding its outcome," wrote Vannoccio Biringuccio in his 1540 book *Pirotechnia,* the first printed volume on metallurgy. "But, with all this, it is a profitable and skillful art and in large part delightful."

Solder for a Quick and Lightweight Joint

Of the several ways of joining metal by using heat, soldering is the simplest, requiring the least heat and heating equipment. But it also forms the weakest joint. Soldering is used to unite thin metals in places where the strength of a welded joint is not needed.

To create this lightweight joint, the metals being joined must be cleaned of all dirt and oxide and must be heated to a temperature high enough to melt the solder completely—usually around 400° F. Solder can be used to bond copper, tin, brass and most steels. Some metals—such as chromium, titanium, magnesium and hardened stainless steel—are difficult to solder. And aluminum can be joined only with a special solder.

Although there are many types of solder, the most common are combinations of lead and tin. For average home use, a solder half tin and half lead—called 50/50 or half-and-half—is recommended. If you do much soldering, you may wish to buy more specialized solders. For instance, a solder of 40 per cent tin and 60 per cent lead is handy for small joints and plumbing connections because it holds better, though it is harder to melt. When the proportions are reversed—60 per cent tin and 40 per cent lead—the solder's lower melting point makes it better for joining electrical components that might be damaged by heat. For small jobs, use solder sold on spoons, called wire solder; for larger joints, solder is also available in rod-shaped bars.

Because solder will not adhere to any oxidized surface, most metals must be cleaned with an oxide-removing agent, called flux, immediately before they are soldered. Flux also improves the solder's ability to flow smoothly over the heated metal. Of the two most common fluxes, rosin and acid flux, the latter—usually made of zinc chloride—removes oxides better. But acid flux corrodes copper and tin badly, so it should not be used in electrical work.

When you use an acid flux, which is caustic and produces toxic fumes, wear gloves and goggles and work only in a well-ventilated area. Most fluxes come in paste form, to be brushed onto the metal surfaces before soldering. But in some cases, fluxes are incorporated into solder as a core, eliminating the need for the preliminary brushing step.

The heat that melts the solder can be applied to the metal surfaces being joined (never directly to the solder), with a hot soldering iron or a propane torch. The iron is suitable for small jobs on flat surfaces; the torch works better for larger jobs and for curved surfaces. A propane torch is always used, for example, to join two sections of copper pipe—a process called sweating (page 63).

Soldering irons come in two forms: Some contain their own electrical heating element; others must be heated over a flame, such as that of a propane torch. A pistol-shaped electric iron, called a soldering gun, has a small tip that heats rapidly, making it useful for work in tight quarters. All soldering irons have copper tips, which must be prepared for soldering by being cleaned with flux, then by being coated with a very thin layer of solder; the latter step is called tinning. This thin coat of solder improves the iron's ability to transfer heat.

The tip of a soldering iron must also be cleaned after each use, to remove burned flux and excess solder (below). In time, the copper tips will be eaten away by the chemical action of the solder and will have to be replaced.

Keep in mind the dangers posed by a hot soldering iron—it can cause a nasty burn or start a fire. When you put a hot tool down, always lay it in its special rack or on a scrap of sheet metal.

Making a Secure Connection with Solder

1 **Cleaning the iron.** Heat the iron, and brush flux onto its tip. Then wipe the tip on a damp sponge to clean off any deposits of solder and oxidation. For stubborn deposits, rub the tip vigorously on a sponge dampened with a half-and-half mixture of water and flux. If the tip is still coated with solder, file it with a mill file (page 16) until the copper surface is shiny.

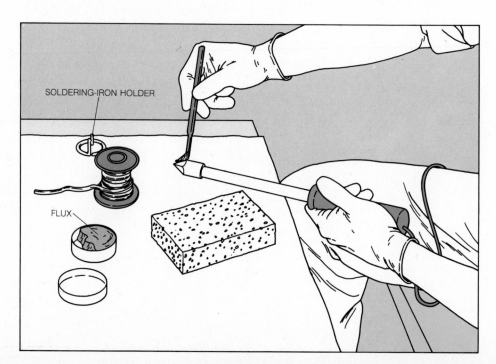

SOLDERING-IRON HOLDER

FLUX

2 **Tinning the iron.** Touch the solder lightly to all the faces on the tip of the soldering iron, coating the tip evenly with a thin layer of solder. Remove excess solder or flux by rubbing the tip lightly on a dampened sponge.

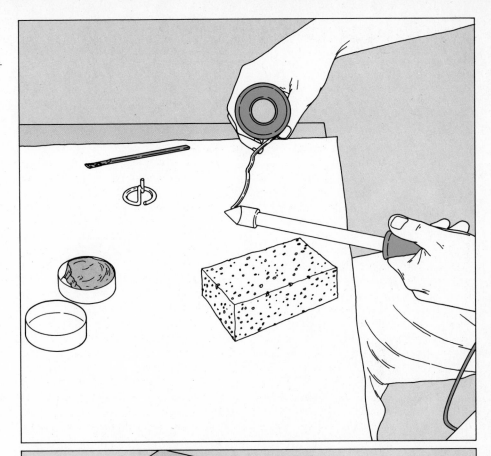

3 **Cleaning and tinning the workpieces.** To remove surface impurities from the workpieces being joined, rub them with steel wool. Then brush them with flux to remove oxidation. Tin one of the pieces by holding the faceted tip of the heated soldering iron flat against the piece, occasionally touching solder to the piece near the tip of the iron until the solder melts and flows evenly. Do not touch the solder to the iron. Move the iron, followed by the solder, along the area of the joint, leaving a thin coat of solder.

After tinning the line of the joint, reheat the piece and wipe over the solder, using a sponge dampened with a half-and-half mixture of flux and water. The result will be a very thin, smooth, shining strip of solder on the workpiece. Tin the other piece in the same way.

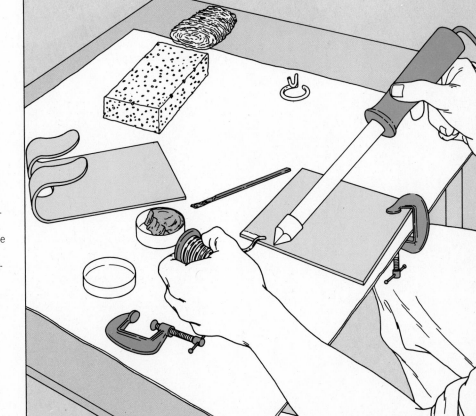

4 **Tacking the joint.** To hold the tinned workpieces together for soldering, clamp them in a vise or secure them with C clamps. Then tack them together with spot soldering. To tack with solder, place the tip of the soldering iron against the top workpiece, slightly behind the joint, and touch the solder to the joint; the solder will be pulled into the joint by capillary action. Continue tacking the joint in the same way until the entire seam is secure.

5 **Soldering the seam.** With the faceted tip of the soldering iron held flat against one end of the seam, gradually move the iron along the seam, heating it and then adding solder to produce a continuous fillet *(inset)*. After the solder has hardened, check it visually for spots where the solder is granular and dull—such spots indicate that it was not heated sufficiently. Resolder these spots, called cold joints, by simply reheating the metal pieces.

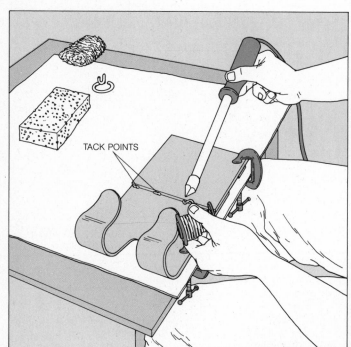

TACK POINTS

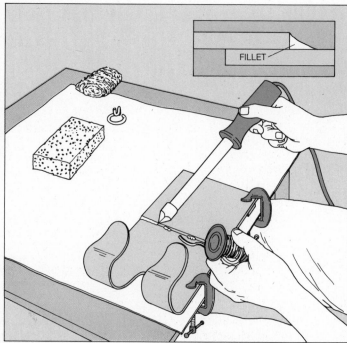

FILLET

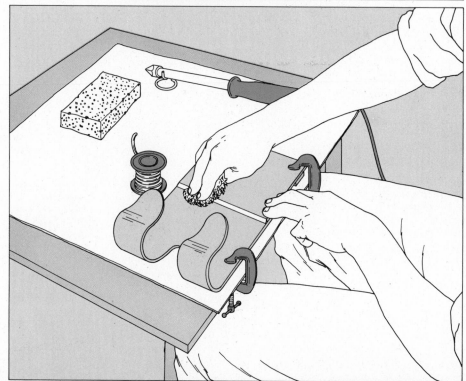

6 **Cleaning the joint.** When it has cooled, rub the soldered joint with steel wool or a soft metal brush to remove the excess flux and leave the joint shining. If the flux contained acid, wash the joint with a mixture of water, detergent and baking soda. Remove any excess driblets of solder with a file or an emery cloth.

Assembling Copper Pipes

Sweating a copper-pipe joint. Clean the ends of the pipe and the fitting with a soft-bristled wire brush or with emery cloth, depending on whether you are dealing with an inside or outside surface. Brush flux onto the cleaned surfaces, assemble the pipe and fitting and twist the two pieces to spread the flux evenly. To solder the joint, heat it with a propane torch and test its temperature by touching solder first to the fitting, then to the pipe. When the solder melts on contact with both surfaces, touch the solder to the pipe where it enters the fitting, and coat the rim of the joint until it is encircled by a ring of solder; the solder will be drawn into the joint by the flux. Repeat to join the ends of each section of pipe and fitting. If there is structural wood near the torch flame, protect the wood with a piece of asbestos board. Wipe off excess solder with a rag while the solder is hot—otherwise it may drip.

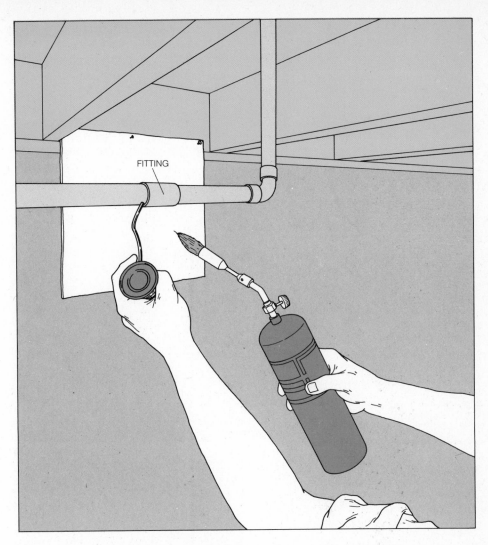

FITTING

A Third-Hand Device for Hard-to-Hold Work

A soldering clamp. Oddly shaped objects that cannot be clamped in an ordinary vise or C clamp can be held with a special soldering clamp that has seven versatile joints. To hold objects of various sizes, the clamp has several sets of adjustable clips that can be unscrewed and replaced with larger or smaller ones.

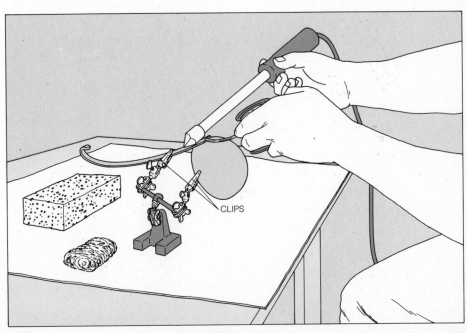

CLIPS

Forging: Shaping Metal with Heat and Hammer

Forging, the shaping of glowing-hot iron or steel with repeated blows of a hammer, is a craft rich in tradition. Once associated with the utilitarian work of the village blacksmith, forging is now primarily used to create decorative objects that can range from custom-designed hardware to ornamental stair rails and fireplace accessories.

The elements essential to forging are a hot fire, an anvil, a water bucket and a double-faced sledge hammer. The metal is heated in the fire to the color appropriate for the job at hand, quickly taken to the anvil, where it is shaped with the hammer, and then immersed in the water bucket for cooling; this immersion is called quenching.

Two basic fires are used in forging. One is the general-purpose fire; the other is a dome-topped, oven-like fire that provides the more intense heat needed for forge welding, a technique for joining metals that produces a strong, almost invisible bond. Both kinds of forging fires, however, should be contained in a 6-inch-deep basin, the forge, with a vent in its bottom or side for propelling air into the fire with a fan or blower. Forges can be purchased, or they can be put together with such familiar components as barbecue grills and vacuum cleaners, depending on the needs and finances of the blacksmith.

Starting and tending the fire are crucial aspects of forging. The fire should be compact, even-burning and almost smokeless—qualities that depend largely on the type of fuel used. The best fuel is soft bituminous coal with granules approximately 1 inch in diameter; it gives the most heat per pound and the least smoke. When wetted and tightly packed during firing, soft coal turns to coke, which burns with great heat and can be saved to start the next fire.

In lieu of soft coal, you can buy coke. You can also substitute hard anthracite coal, although hard coal does not produce as much heat as soft coal, and it is therefore not suitable for forge welding. In a pinch you can even build a forging fire from charcoal or charcoal briquets. However, they are expensive forms of heat because they are consumed more quickly than coal. With any forging fire, it is best to cut off the air blast as soon as metal has reached the desired color, in order to conserve fuel.

The anvil on which the metal is shaped should be made of cast steel. Although a section of railroad rail makes an adequate substitute, an anvil made especially for forging has many more features for shaping metal. Its rectangular work surface, the face, has one squared edge and one

Forging Temperatures Gauged by Metal Colors

Forging colors and temperatures. The chart at right shows the range of colors through which iron and steel pass when heated to between 1,200° and 2,550° F., the temperatures needed for forging. Heat affects both metals similarly: Their crystalline structure expands, causing the metal to weaken and become plastic. The degree of plasticity needed varies with the particular forging operation being performed.

Color in metal not only indicates its readiness for working, but is also a gauge used in quenching. When metals are quenched, they should be returned to at least dark cherry red; otherwise the reserve heat will cause the metal fibers to reexpand, weakening and softening the workpiece. In addition, at certain colors steel takes on characteristic behaviors. When it is light cherry red, a crust, or scale, appears on its surface. When it is orange, the scale flakes off the workpiece in the form of brittle ash.

Color	Temperature	Forging Characteristics
Dark cherry red	1,200° to 1,300° F.	Lower limit of forging. Light surface shaping possible.
Cherry red	1,420° to 1,460° F.	Quenching temperature.
Light cherry red	1,600° to 1,620° F.	Curves and angle can be formed. This heat is required for upsetting welding joints. Scale forms.
Orange	1,775° F.	Work can be sheared over hardie. This heat is required for drawing out. Scale flakes off.
Yellow	2,000° to 2,350° F.	Holes can be punched. This heat is required for upsetting.
Incandescent white	2,350° to 2,500° F.	Welding is possible at upper range; some sparks.
Fiery white	2,550° F.	Welding heat; upper forging limit. Sparks explode from metal, and work is difficult to look at directly.

rounded edge along its length. The squared edge can be used to shape an exact 90° angle.

At one end of the rectangular work surface, the anvil is undercut, forming a tail over which various acute angles can be shaped. Also in the tail are two holes—a round hole, the pritchel hole, about ⅜ inch in diameter, which is used for bending rods and punching holes; and a square hole, from ⅝ to 1¼ inches across, into which a chisel-edged cutting tool, called a cut-off hardie, is mounted. With the cut-off hardie, heated pieces of metal up to 1½ inches across can be sheared in two. Protruding from the opposite end of the anvil is a rounded snout, known as the horn, on which various curves can be shaped.

Among the shaping techniques used in forging are two that have special applications: metal wrapping and metal piercing. The former uses a rod and a forging hammer with a wedge-shaped head, the cross-peen, to create the circular eye needed for hinges. The latter makes use of the anvil's pritchel hole and metal punches of various sizes and configurations to punch holes through metal up to 2 inches thick.

Other forging techniques commonly used include two that transform metal's dimensions. In one, called upsetting, a section of metal is thickened by compressing the metal's length. Upsetting is normally done on the anvil, with a hammer, but you can upset a longer piece of metal by holding it in both hands—adequately gloved, of course—and thumping it against a concrete floor; protect the floor from the hot metal with a piece of sheet metal.

Drawing out elongates and thins a metal rod or bar. Both upsetting and drawing out can be done at any point along the piece of metal, so the contouring possibilities are endless. And in drawing out, the shape of the piece in cross section—whether it is to be square, round, rectangular or oval—is controlled by the placement of the hammer blows.

Cadence is an important part of the metal-shaping process. The good blacksmith establishes a beat, striking the workpiece and allowing the hammer to bounce, then bouncing it a second time, off the face of the anvil, developing momentum. The striking trajectories have a practical purpose. The effortless upstroke makes the work less tiring, and the regularity of the downstroke improves the accuracy of the blows.

As with other metalworking methods involving heat, safety attire is imperative when forging. A full-length apron made of leather or heavy canvas and a shatterproof face shield are necessary for protection from flying fragments of hot metal. You will also need leather-palmed work gloves for handling hot metal at the forge and on the anvil. For gripping a piece of metal that is shorter than 18 inches, use universal forging tongs or any long-handled tongs suited to the shape of the specific piece.

Workroom for a Blacksmith

A basic shop for forging. The forge and the anvil form the heart of this well-designed blacksmith shop. Located close to them are a workbench, a water barrel and a coal bin. This set-up saves walking with materials that often are hot and heavy. The forge is vented outdoors, much like a woodstove, with a metal hood mounted 30 to 36 inches above the hearth; a 6- or 8-inch stovepipe removes smoke. On the plywood coal bin are hooks and a rack for tool storage.

The anvil should be 4 to 5 feet from the forge and bolted securely to a stable base; here a hardwood log serves as an anvil mount. The mount should raise the face, or top, of the anvil to a height equal to the height of your knuckles above the floor when your arms are at your sides. The water barrel—a galvanized-metal garbage can—should be placed near the anvil and forge, for quenching hot workpieces. A sturdy metal-topped workbench supports heavy workpieces during layout and provides a mounting place for a metalworking vise. Wall-mounted racks store steel and iron supplies out of the work area.

An indoor blacksmith shop should have a concrete floor, and the workbench area should be well lighted. However, illumination on the forge and anvil should be fairly low, to allow an accurate assessment of the color of heated metal. In addition to smoke removal, heat removal by an exhaust fan is essential, to relieve the excessive forge-produced heat.

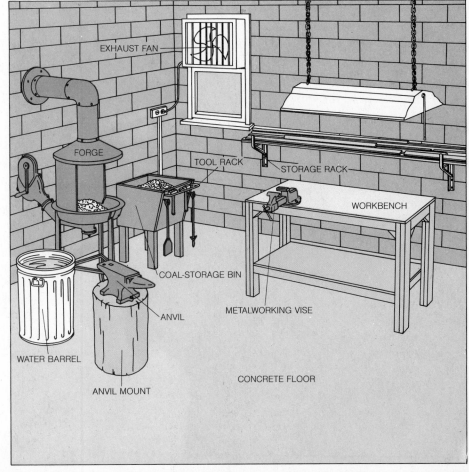

EXHAUST FAN

FORGE

TOOL RACK

STORAGE RACK

WORKBENCH

METALWORKING VISE

COAL-STORAGE BIN

ANVIL

WATER BARREL

ANVIL MOUNT

CONCRETE FLOOR

Building a Fire Hot Enough for Forging

A fire for general-purpose forging. Place an empty one-pound coffee can, bottom up, over the air grate in the bottom of the forge, and pack a ring of coal about 5 inches high completely around the can. Remove the coffee can and in its place build a small, loose stack of kindling mixed with strips of paper. Ignite the paper strips and, as they burn, send a small air blast through them with the forge blower. Drop bits of coal onto the fire and, as it burns, sprinkle water on the coal packed closest around the fire. This, combined with the heat of the fire, will make the coal stick together and form coke, a brittle dark-gray mass that burns evenly with little or no smoke. As the fire consumes the coke, pull in more coal and sprinkle it, while adding fresh coal around the fire's edge.

From time to time, examine the glowing hot coke for any dark areas. These areas indicate bits of coal that are not burning; blacksmiths call them clinkers. They are the result of impurities and are harder than pure coal. Clinkers will cause uneven heat; remove them with tongs or a poker and set them aside in the forge basin.

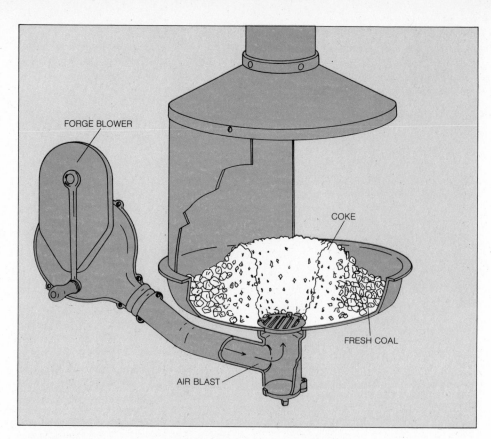

FORGE BLOWER

COKE

FRESH COAL

AIR BLAST

An Anvil-mounted Chisel for Cutting Hot Metal

Using a cut-off hardie. Heat the workpiece until the area to be cut is orange, then position the cut-off point over the edge of the cut-off hardie. Hammer the workpiece with heavy blows directly over the hardie until a thin, dark line appears across the metal, indicating that the metal has been cooled by contact with the unheated hardie. Continue hammering the metal, but with lighter blows to avoid breaking through the workpiece and damaging the hardie's cutting edge. When the metal is almost severed, strike one or two medium blows just next to the hardie, at the free end of the workpiece *(inset);* the piece will snap in two.

Alternatively, you can complete the cut by quenching the workpiece just before the metal is severed, then breaking the thin, brittle sliver of remaining metal. At this point you can either break the piece by hand or rest the free end over the edge of the anvil and tap it with a hammer.

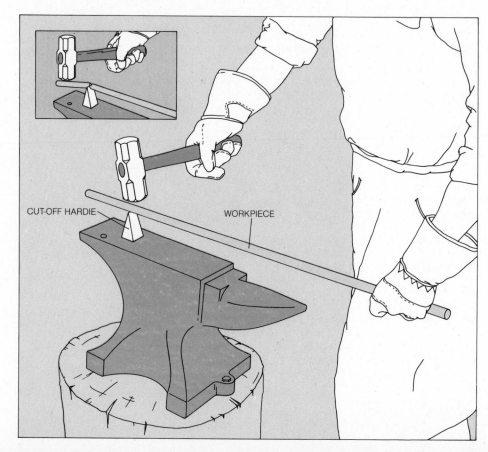

CUT-OFF HARDIE

WORKPIECE

Angle Forming with the Edge of the Anvil

Shaping a 90° angle. Heat the workpiece to a light cherry red for several inches on both sides of the point to be bent. Then hold the workpiece across the anvil, tilting it up 10° or 15°, with the bend line resting on the squared edge of the anvil. With the workpiece gripped firmly, hammer the overhanging end against the side of the anvil. As this end approaches the anvil side, gradually lower the other end and alternately strike first one end, then the other, until both lie flat, one against the anvil face, the other against the anvil side *(inset)*.

To remove the indentations caused by the hammer blows, strike the metal with lighter blows all over the irregular areas, until the surface of the workpiece regains its shape.

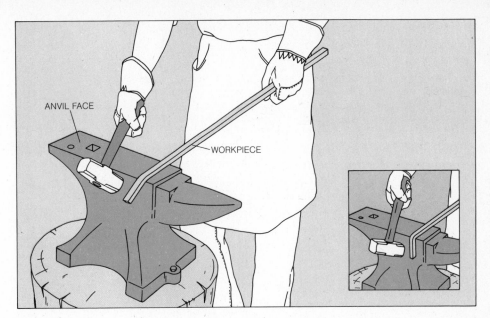

ANVIL FACE

WORKPIECE

Open or Tight Curves Shaped on an Anvil

ANVIL HORN

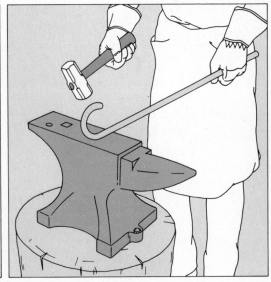

1 **Using the anvil horn as a form.** Heat the workpiece to a light cherry red and lay it across the horn. When curving the end of the workpiece, heat the tip enough to overhang the horn by 2 or 3 inches. When curving along the shaft, heat an area sufficient to straddle the horn 2 or 3 inches on both sides.

To curve the end of the workpiece, hammer its tip against the horn *(inset);* then gradually push the piece away from you, continuing to hammer over the far side of the horn. If necessary, reheat the workpiece and alter its position on the horn until you achieve the desired curve.

To curve the workpiece at a point along the shaft, use the same hammer technique used to bend an end, but have an assistant support the other end of the workpiece if necessary.

2 **Freehand finishing a tight curve.** To tighten a curved end into a hook, place the workpiece across the anvil face, curved end facing up; if necessary, reheat the piece to a light cherry red. Hammer the tip of the curved end down toward the shaft until it reaches the desired shape—an open crook or a closed circle.

A Classic Technique for Making Hardware

Shaping an eye for a hinge pin. Place a metal strip, heated to a light cherry red, across the anvil, with the end of the strip overhanging the rounded edge of the anvil as shown. Measure the amount of overhang while the strip is still cold: Subtract the thickness of the strip from the diameter of the rod that is going to be used to form the eye, then multiply the resulting figure by 3.14 and measure this distance inward from the end of the strip. Use a triangular file to make a small notch in the edge of the strip at this point. After heating the strip, position the notch on the edge of the anvil and hammer the end of the strip over the anvil *(below, left)*.

Lay the strip, bend up, on the anvil *(below, right)*, reheated if necessary. While a helper holds the strip, put a rod of the right diameter in the crook of the bend. Hammer the end of the strip tightly around the rod, using the wedge head of a cross-peen hammer. Turn the rod occasionally, to keep it from fusing with the strip.

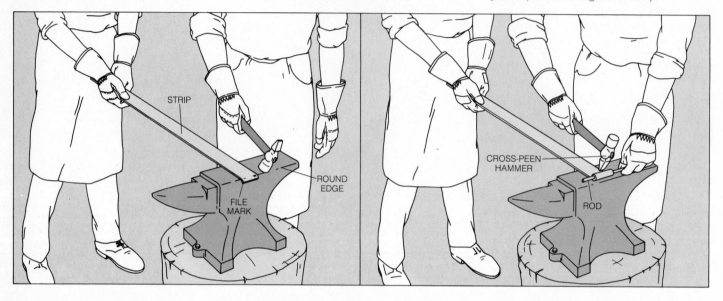

Making a Metal Shaft Thicker by Upsetting It

Upsetting a workpiece. To thicken the end of a shaft, bring the end to a yellow heat and hold the shaft upright, heated end down, on the anvil face. Using a gloved hand to hold the shaft, or tongs if it is shorter than 18 inches, strike the upper end of the shaft with a hammer. Adjust the force of your blows to produce the degree of thickening desired. Work quickly, because the metal becomes harder to shape the moment it is withdrawn from the fire. When the shaft has swollen to the desired shape, lay it across the face of the anvil and use hammer blows to correct any inconsistencies in its contours.

To thicken a specific area along the shaft *(inset)*, heat the shaft up to and including that area, bringing it to an orange color. Then cool the heated end in water, hardening it so that only the desired area will thicken during the upsetting process. Shape the shaft as described above.

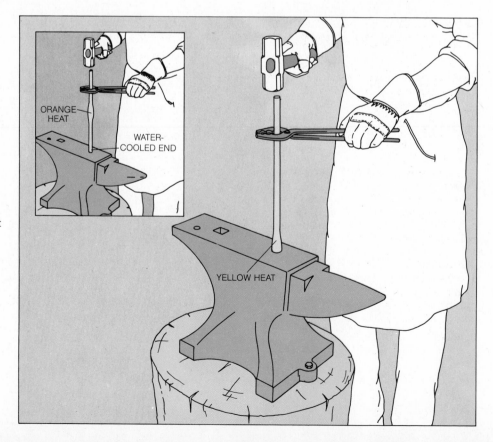

Elongating a Shaft by Drawing It Out

Drawing out a workpiece. To lengthen a shaft and reduce its diameter, heat its end to an orange color and place it across the anvil. Hold it at an angle of 10° to 15° to the anvil face and allow it to extend slightly beyond the anvil edge *(below, left)*. Hammer the tip with medium blows over the anvil edge, while slowly pushing the piece away from you. Continue to hammer over the anvil edge; in effect, what you are doing is squeezing the piece between the hammer and the edge of the anvil. Turn the workpiece over and repeat the process, to smooth out the impressions left by the anvil edge and to straighten the slight bend in the tip left by the initial hammering. When both sides of the piece are flat, hammer them lightly to remove any irregularities in their surface. Draw out the two remaining rounded sides, as before *(below, center)*.

If the finished piece is to be rounded, reheat it to an orange color, return it to the anvil and hammer the corners as you progress *(below, right)*. Lighten your hammer blows as you approach the desired thickness and length.

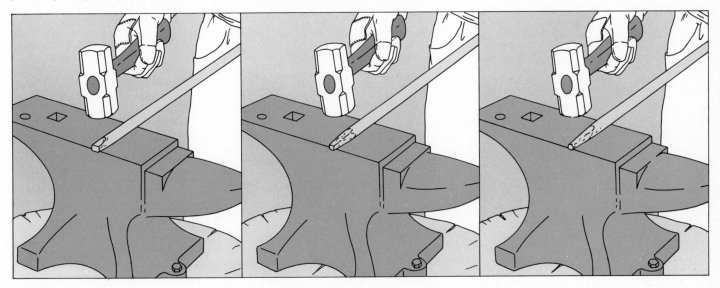

A Punch-and-Anvil Method of Making Holes

Using a special tool to pierce metal. Mark the center of the proposed hole with a center punch, then heat the metal until it is yellow. Have a helper hold the piece against the tail of the anvil, lining up the punch mark with the pritchel hole. Place the metal punch on this mark and strike it heavily and repeatedly with the hammer, driving the punch about three-quarters of the way through the metal. Quench the tip of the punch with every third blow, to prevent it from becoming hot enough to stick to the hot workpiece. If the workpiece is thicker than 1 inch, you will probably have to reheat it.

Turn the workpiece over and again position it over the pritchel hole, using the bulge of the partially punched hole as a guide. Strike the punch sharply with the hammer to drive the remaining slug of metal out of the workpiece and through the pritchel hole.

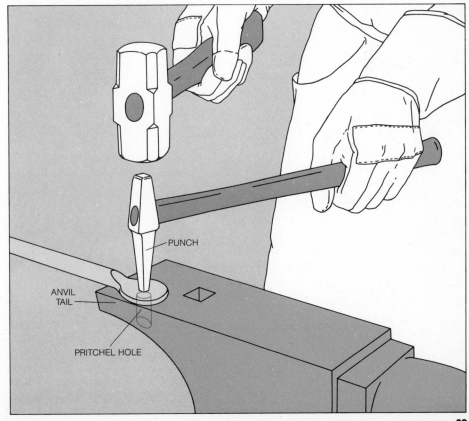

Forge Welding with a Superheated Fire

1 Building a fire for intense heat. Construct a bowl-shaped coal-and-coke fire as shown on page 66. When the fire is formed, place one end of a 6-inch length of 2-by-4 or 4-by-4 lumber in the center of the fire, resting the outer end of the lumber on the edge of the bowl. Pack fresh coal completely over the lumber, enclosing it in a dome of coal; then sprinkle the dome with water. The lumber will burn away, leaving a hole in the side of the dome through which workpieces may be passed. The fire within the dome, contained and intensified, will reach the temperature that is required for welding.

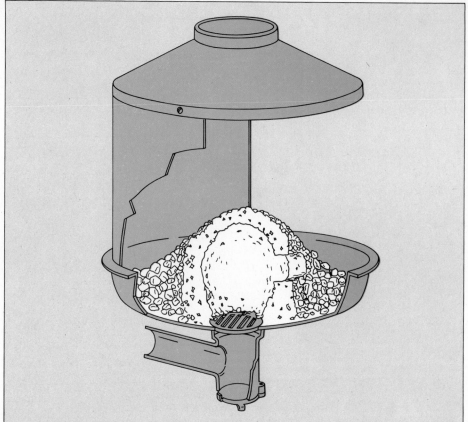

2 Upsetting a welding bevel. Heat the end of the workpiece to be welded to a light cherry red, and place it across the face of the anvil. With hammer blows, shape the end of the workpiece into a slightly bulging bevel. Heat and form the other piece to be welded in the same fashion. If you are working with steel, sprinkle a flux of one part borax and four parts silicon sand on the beveled surfaces; iron needs no flux. Return both workpieces to the fire and slowly increase the air blast until the flames are fiery white; the fire will be so bright it will be hard to look at.

When you think the workpieces have risen to welding temperature, push into the fire a thin metal test rod, ¼ inch in diameter at the most. The rod should be of the same metal as the workpieces. Touch the heated workpieces with the test rod; if they are hot enough for welding, the rod will tend to stick to them.

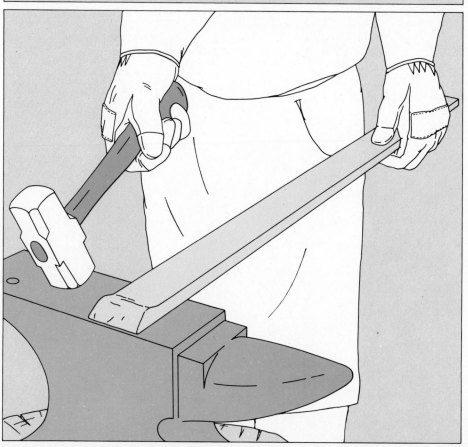

3 Hammering the weld. Have a helper remove one of the workpieces from the fire while you remove the other; quickly move both to the anvil. Small sparks will be exploding from the metal since it is at welding heat. Lay one piece across the anvil, bevel up, and immediately but carefully place the other piece on top of it, bevel down, overlapping the bevels *(inset).* It is good practice to rehearse your moves together before the workpieces are fired to welding heat. Strike both pieces quickly and sharply with the hammer at the center of the overlap, to anchor the weld. Then strike the overlap with two lighter blows, to the right and the left of the first blow, along the center of the joint. Turn the pieces over, and repeat the same hammer pattern on the other side. To finish the weld, hammer over the entire weld seam on both sides, closing the joint and forcing out the flux as the rounded surfaces of the bevels flatten together.

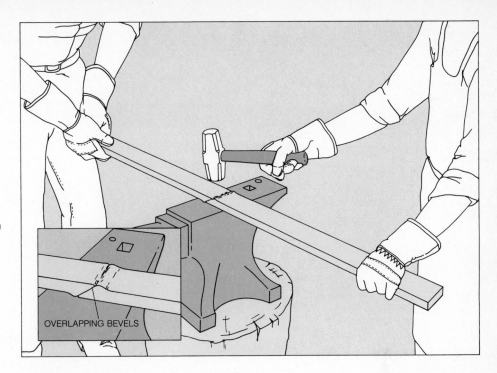

OVERLAPPING BEVELS

Building a Forge from an Old Barbecue Grill

This inexpensive forge, suitable for use outdoors by an amateur blacksmith, is made from an old barbecue grill with legs sturdy enough to support the weights that forging involves. If the grill bottom is badly rusted, it can be reinforced with a lining of ⅛-inch sheet metal, fastened to the still-sound parts with sheet-metal screws or rivets.

A 2½- to 3-inch steel pipe flange is attached to the center of the bottom with nuts and bolts; air holes, to feed air to the fire, are drilled into the bottom over the flange opening. A steel pipe nipple is screwed into the flange, followed in sequence by a steel T fitting, a brass nipple and a steel pipe cap. The brass nipple prevents the intense heat of the forge from fusing the cap to the pipe, which would interfere with its removal for emptying ashes.

Steel pipe connects the T fitting to a forge blower, which can be hand-powered or electric-powered, or to an improvised blower such as a vacuum cleaner. Pipe connectors and blast gates are available for connecting forge blowers but you may have to improvise your own. A styrofoam cup with a perforated bottom can be set into a pipe extension

at least 18 inches away from the T fitting, for example, to serve as an adaptor for a plastic vacuum-cleaner hose.

For optimum efficiency, the forge should have a sheet-metal windscreen

attached with sheet-metal screws or rivets. The bottom of the pan should be protected from the oxidizing effect of intense heat by a 1-inch layer of potter's clay or vermiculite.

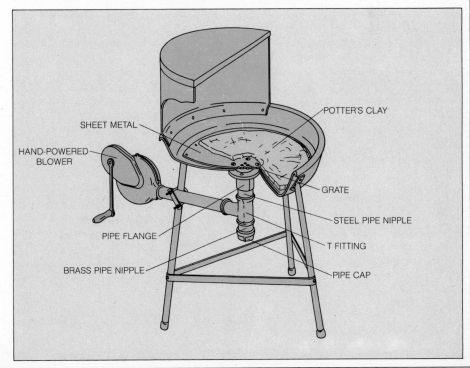

SHEET METAL

HAND-POWERED BLOWER

POTTER'S CLAY

GRATE

STEEL PIPE NIPPLE

T FITTING

PIPE CAP

PIPE FLANGE

BRASS PIPE NIPPLE

An Oxyacetylene Torch for Welding and Cutting

Although an oxyacetylene rig does not weld as quickly and easily as an electric arc-welding machine *(page 86)*, for most homeowners it is a more practical apparatus because it is mobile and more versatile. A lightweight assembly of gas tanks, gauges and valves, the rig rolls around a workshop floor on a hand truck, and its wandlike torch has talents other than welding: Its 6,000° F. flame, a burning mixture of oxygen and acetylene, can also cut metal *(page 81)* and heat it for bending *(page 84)*.

Welding with an oxyacetylene torch, like all welding, fuses two pieces of metal together to make a finished joint as strong as the original metal. A third piece of metal, called a filler rod or welding rod and available at welding-supply stores, is sometimes used in the welding process to build up the seam for even greater strength. When purchasing a filler rod, check with the supplier to make certain that its metal is compatible with the two pieces being joined.

Oxyacetylene rigs come in sizes based on the capacity of the oxygen and acetylene cylinders, which hold from 10 to more than 400 cubic feet. Be sure to get regulators, valves and hoses that match the cylinder sizes selected. Unless you expect to use the equipment a great deal, 20 cubic feet each of oxygen and acetylene—enough to weld for one hour or cut for 20 minutes—is ample. The equipment can be bought at welding-supply stores or rented from tool-rental agencies listed in classified directories under "Welding Equipment—Renting." If you choose to buy the equipment, the tanks may be empty when you get them; have them filled at a welding-supply shop.

When you rent an oxyacetylene rig, welding or cutting tips in a range of sizes for different metal thicknesses are usually available. Buying tips individually can be confusing, since each of the dozens of tip manufacturers uses a different numbering system; to buy the right size, you must consult a size chart for a specific brand. The same chart prescribes the pressure to be set on the oxygen and acetylene gauges for each size tip.

If you are welding for the first time, begin by practicing puddling, a technique basic to all welding; it consists of moving a puddle of molten metal with the torch flame. After mastering this action, practice puddling with a filler rod. Next, try your hand at tacking, the technique of temporarily joining two pieces at one point to hold them in alignment during the next step, welding. Finally, practice each of the four basic welds: the butt, the T, the lap and the corner joint.

Butt and lap joints are for joining pieces along a straight edge and can often be used interchangeably. A lap joint is easier to make and provides greater contact area, but a butt joint is flush and is easier to grind smooth and conceal. When a butt joint is used to join two pieces of metal thicker than 1/8 inch, the edges of the two pieces must first be beveled with a cutting torch to get a weld that reaches the bottom of the joint. For the T and corner joints, which join pieces of metal at a right angle, a pair of locking-grip pliers is needed to hold the upright piece in place as you tack the pieces together. To ensure even melting, the four joints require slightly different positions for the torch and the filler rod.

When the weld is complete, the metal is often dressed, or finished, with a disk sander-grinder, which can be purchased or rented. Various grits are available for smoothing metal, rounding contours, removing nicks, burrs and rust, and preparing metal for painting. Wear goggles when you use a sander-grinder (it sends off showers of debris and sparks), and anchor the work securely in a vise.

In addition to welding, an oxyacetylene torch can be used for brazing, a special technique that joins dissimilar metals by melting a brass or bronze filler rod between them. A brazed joint is made more quickly but is somewhat weaker than a welded joint. Cleanliness of the surfaces is critical: They must be sanded with a sander-grinder and the debris wiped off; and the filler rod must be either prefluxed by the manufacturer or heated and inserted in flux, to dissolve oxidation on the surfaces being joined.

In brazing, the two metals are heated to a dull red, and the tip of the filler rod is touched to them, melting as it flows along the joint. If the metal is not hot enough, the filler will roll off in a ball; if it is too hot, the puddle will smoke. Never melt the rod directly in the flame.

When you use an oxyacetylene torch—whether to weld, cut, bend or braze—safety is of the utmost importance. Along with the safe working procedures listed at right, proper dress and a hazard-free workshop are essential. Always protect your eyes with welding goggles or a tinted face mask to screen out ultraviolet and infrared rays; wear gloves and a flame-resistant shop coat or apron, or coveralls without cuffs. All welding should be done in a well-ventilated area to prevent the accumulation of toxic fumes, and away from any materials that are flammable.

The work should be supported on firebricks above an all-metal worktable. Suspend the metal between the firebricks rather than placing it on a solid firebrick base—otherwise the silicone in the firebricks may melt and fuse with the metal. And do not weld on concrete, cement or asphalt—the moisture in those materials may expand under heat and cause them to explode.

The welding equipment itself must also be protected from damage by the recognition of two common mechanical failures, backfire and flashback. A backfire, the unexpected extinguishing of the flame, is often accompanied by a loud popping sound. It is caused by touching the torch tip against the work, by using a dirty or clogged tip, or by operating the equipment at the wrong pressures. When a backfire occurs, quickly shut down the rig and check the tip and the pressure gauges. A set of metal tip cleaners is useful for dislodging carbon from a clogged tip, and brushing it with steel wool will remove external dirt.

In flashback, a different problem with similar causes, the flame disappears from the tip but the gas continues to burn inside the torch or the hoses. Flashback begins with a loud popping sound, followed by shrill hissing. It can be caused by using a tip of the wrong size, by operating the equipment at the wrong pressure, or by allowing the tip to touch the work. When flashback occurs, turn off the gases and inspect the rig for damage. Clean it up and restart the torch. If it does not work, take it to the equipment supplier and have it checked.

Anatomy of an oxyacetylene rig. Two cylinders—a tall one containing oxygen and a shorter one containing acetylene—stand on a two-wheel hand cart, chained together to keep them from tipping over. The acetylene cylinder's valve is opened by means of a T wrench on top, the oxygen cylinder's valve by means of a knob. When not in use, each valve is covered with a protective cap that screws onto the neck of the cylinder.

At the side of each valve a dual regulator, with two gauges, measures the pressure in the cylinder and the working pressure in the hose. The working pressure is adjusted by means of the T screw on the front of each regulator. Separate hoses—a red one for acetylene and a green or black one for oxygen—carry the gases to the torch *(inset)*, where an oxygen valve and an acetylene valve control the proportion of each gas at the tip of the torch.

Safety Rules for Welding

☐ Always store the cylinders in an upright position.
☐ Never move the cylinders without their protective caps in place.
☐ Do not let oil or grease come in contact with oxygen cylinders, valves, regulators, gauges or fittings.
☐ Do not stand in front of the cylinder nozzles when opening the valves.
☐ Always open the gas valves slowly, and never open the acetylene valve more than a half turn.
☐ Leave the acetylene cylinder's T wrench in place so that the valve can be closed quickly in an emergency.
☐ Never light the torch with a match; always use a spark lighter *(page 76)*.
☐ Never let the acetylene working pressure exceed 15 pounds per square inch; at pressures greater than this, the gas can explode.
☐ When putting down the torch for a few minutes, first turn off the torch valves; shut down the rig completely when you are finished.
☐ If you smell acetylene, an explosive gas with a strong, nauseating odor, shut down the rig at once and try to locate the leak *(page 75)*. Call the supplier if you cannot solve the problem.

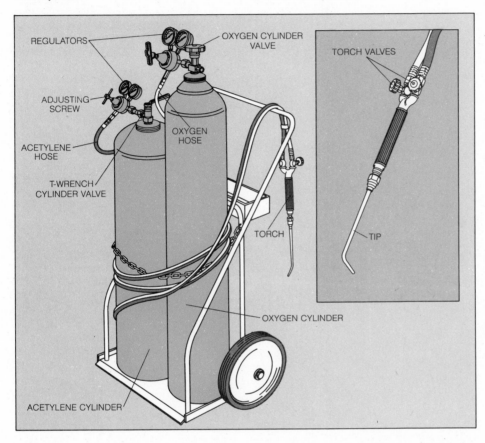

Setting Up a Rig for Welding

1 **Clearing the valves.** Remove the acetylene cylinder's protective cap, and stand so that the valve outlet nozzle points away from you. Open the valve slightly by turning the T wrench about a quarter turn counterclockwise. After one second, close the valve by turning it clockwise. Wipe out the inside of the valve nozzle to remove dirt from the seat of the regulator.

Remove the protective cap of the oxygen cylinder and repeat the process to clear the oxygen valve. Again, wipe out the inside of the nozzle.

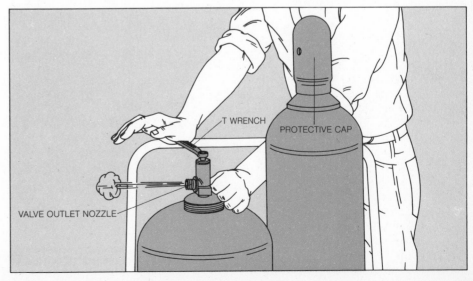

2 **Attaching the regulators.** Turn the adjusting screw of the acetylene regulator counterclockwise until you feel no resistance. Put the regulator fitting inside the valve nozzle, and tighten the regulator nut first by hand, then with a wrench, until it is very snug. Attach the oxygen regulator by following the same steps.

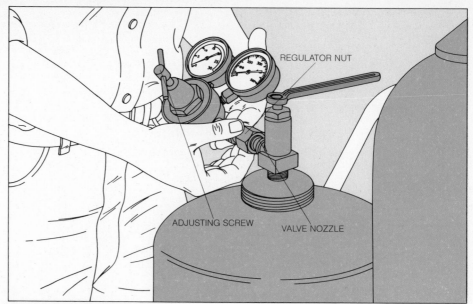

REGULATOR NUT

ADJUSTING SCREW   VALVE NOZZLE

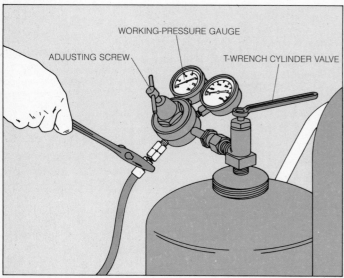

WORKING-PRESSURE GAUGE

ADJUSTING SCREW   T-WRENCH CYLINDER VALVE

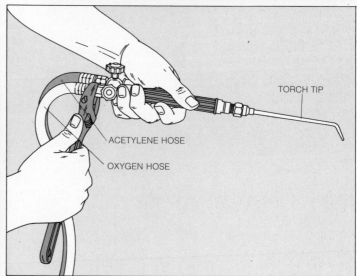

TORCH TIP

ACETYLENE HOSE

OXYGEN HOSE

3 **Attaching the hoses.** Connect the red hose to the acetylene regulator and the green or black hose to the oxygen regulator. The acetylene fitting on the hose is notched on the hose fitting and is screwed on counterclockwise; the oxygen hose fitting is screwed on clockwise.

If the hoses are new, they may be lined with talcum powder, which should be blown out. To do this, grasp the free ends of both hoses in one hand and point them away from you. Slowly open the acetylene cylinder valve, and then turn the adjusting screw of the regulator clockwise until the working-pressure gauge of the regulator reads 10 pounds. After about two seconds, close the adjusting screw and the cylinder valve. Blow out the oxygen hose in the same way, opening the cylinder valve and turning the regulator's adjusting screw on the oxygen cylinder to bring the working-pressure gauge to 10 pounds. Then close the screw and valve.

4 **Assembling the torch and tip.** Select the tip you plan to use, and screw it onto the torch end. Connect the red hose to the torch nozzle marked FUEL or GAS, and the green or black oxygen hose to the nozzle marked OXY. Turn the acetylene hose nut counterclockwise and the oxygen hose nut clockwise. Tighten both of the nuts with a wrench.

Check to see if the tip is clean. If it is not, insert a metal tip cleaner slightly smaller than the hole, guiding it carefully into the hole in a straight line so that you will not damage the opening. Graduate to a tip cleaner the same size as the hole, and repeat the cleaning process.

5 **Checking for leaks.** To make sure the torch valves are closed, turn the oxygen and acetylene valves clockwise. Then stand to one side and slowly open the oxygen cylinder valve one half turn *(below, left)*. Turn the adjusting screw until the oxygen working-pressure gauge reads 20 pounds. Then open the acetylene cylinder valve a quarter turn, and turn the adjusting screw until the acetylene working-pressure gauge reads 5 pounds. Close both cylinder valves, and watch the cylinder-pressure gauges; if they fall, there is a leak. Repeat Steps 2 through 4, tightening all the fittings, then repeat the test.

If tightening the fittings does not solve the problem, locate the leak by brushing all the fit- tings and the hoses with a soapy solution made by mixing a capful of liquid dishwashing detergent in a gallon of water *(below, right)*. (Do not use soap containing lanolin or oil.) Bubbles will appear at the leak. If a fitting leaks beyond correction, return it to the supplier for replacement. After a successful leak test, reset the regulators for the correct tip pressure.

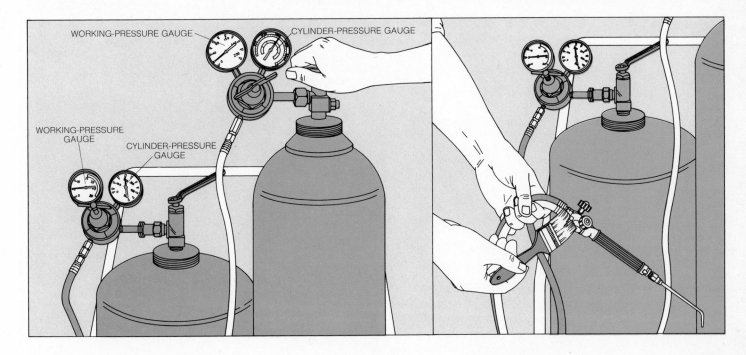

WORKING-PRESSURE GAUGE

CYLINDER-PRESSURE GAUGE

WORKING-PRESSURE GAUGE

CYLINDER-PRESSURE GAUGE

Shutting Down a Welding Rig

1 **Draining the lines.** Turn off both torch valves—first the acetylene, then the oxygen—and then close the acetylene and oxygen cylinder valves. Open the acetylene torch valve until both regulator gauges on the acetylene cylinder read 0, then shut the acetylene torch valve. Drain the oxygen line in the same way.

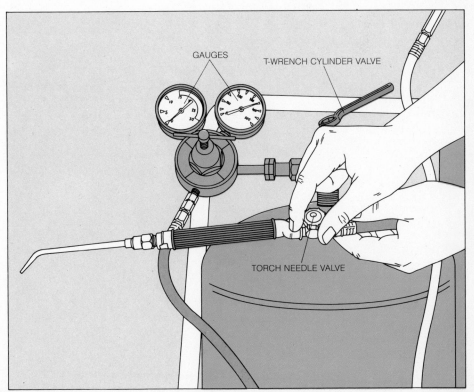

GAUGES

T-WRENCH CYLINDER VALVE

TORCH NEEDLE VALVE

2 **Releasing the adjusting screws.** Turn the adjusting screw of the acetylene regulator counterclockwise until you feel no resistance. Then do the same with the adjusting screw of the oxygen regulator, turning it counterclockwise. Coil the hoses, and drape them over the cart so that they will not drag on the floor. Place the torch on the shelf on the back of the cart.

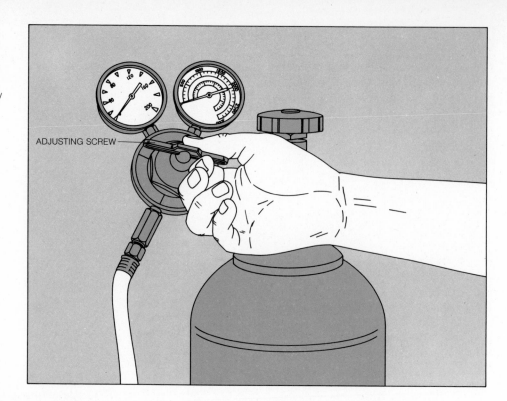

ADJUSTING SCREW

How to Light and Adjust the Torch Flame

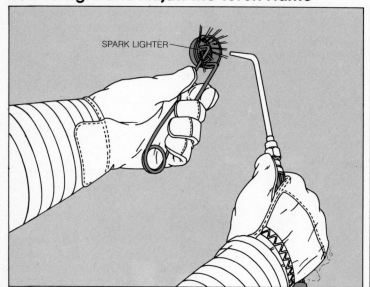

SPARK LIGHTER

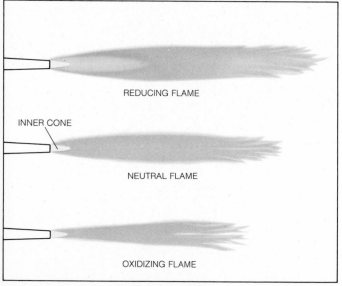

INNER CONE

REDUCING FLAME

NEUTRAL FLAME

OXIDIZING FLAME

1 **Lighting the torch.** Open the acetylene cylinder valve a quarter turn and the oxygen cylinder valve all the way. Turn the regulator adjusting screws until the working pressures on the regulator gauges match the pressures that are recommended for the size tip you are using. Open the acetylene torch valve about a three-quarter turn, and hold the spark lighter approximately an inch away from the torch tip, to ignite the acetylene. If the flame is smoky, add more acetylene until the smoke disappears; at this point, the base of the flame ought to be just barely touching the torch tip.

2 **Adjusting the flame.** Slowly open the oxygen torch valve until a well-defined bluish-white inner cone appears near the torch tip. Adjust the valve to get what is called a neutral flame *(above, center),* with a rounded inner cone of light blue. Excess oxygen yields an oxidizing flame, with a pointed inner cone and a shorter envelope *(above, bottom);* it will overheat the metal, causing holes in the weld. Too little oxygen yields a reducing flame with two inner cones, one small and rounded, one large and shadowy with a feathered edge *(above, top);* it will introduce carbon into the metal, creating a brittle weld.

The Basic Technique: Forming and Moving Puddles

Forming and moving a puddle. Lay a piece of 1/16- or 1/8-inch-thick metal stock on top of two firebricks. Light the torch and adjust it for a neutral flame. Hold the torch tip at a 90° angle to the metal, with the inner cone of the flame about 1/16 inch above the metal surface, until a circular puddle of metal forms (below, left). Then tilt the torch tip sideways about 15° and,

with a circular motion, move the puddle forward about 1/8 inch at a time in the direction the tip is pointing (below, right). Continue the circling movement to carry the molten puddle across the metal. If the puddle digs too deeply into the metal, move the torch forward faster. If the puddle is small and irregular in outline, correct it by moving the torch more slowly.

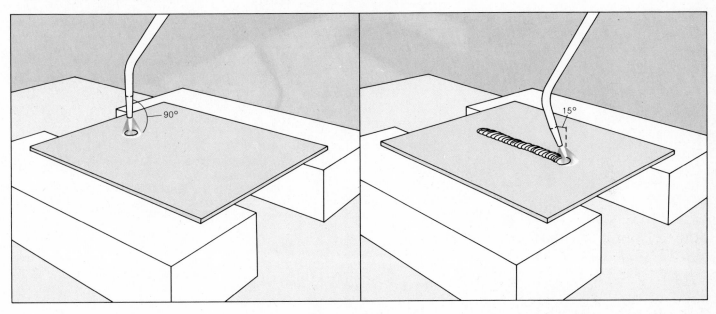

Building With Filler Rods

Puddling with a filler rod. Select a rod of the same diameter as the thickness of the metal plate, and heat the plate until a puddle forms. Tilt the torch and begin puddling. At the same time, insert the tip of the filler rod into the center of the puddle, holding the rod at the same angle as the torch but slanted in the opposite direction. Advance the torch with a circular motion, keeping the tip of the rod just in front of it. Raise and lower the rod into the puddle as necessary, in order to build up an even band of metal slightly higher than the plate around it.

When you raise the rod out of the puddle, keep its tip just inside the flame, so that the rod does not cool and harden. If the tip of the rod sticks in the puddle, do not jerk it loose; instead, play the flame directly on the rod until it melts enough so that it can be freed gently.

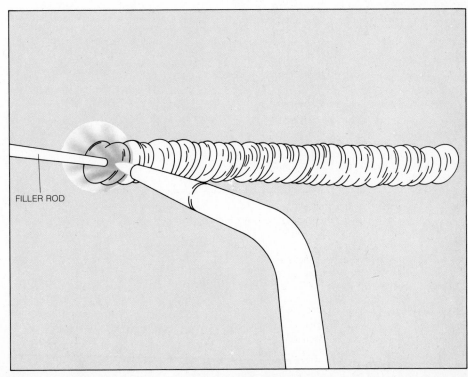

FILLER ROD

How to Weld a Butt Joint

1 **Tacking the pieces.** Place the two pieces of metal that are to be joined flush with each other about 1/16 inch apart on the two spaced firebricks. Light the torch, adjust it for a neutral flame and hold the flame over the center of the joint, moving the torch in a small circle. When the metal begins to melt, touch the joint with the filler rod, melting the parent metal and filler rod into one puddle. Continue to move the torch in a circle. When the pieces are tacked together, withdraw the torch, and tack-weld each end of the joint. Then make intermediate tack welds every 4 to 5 inches along the joint.

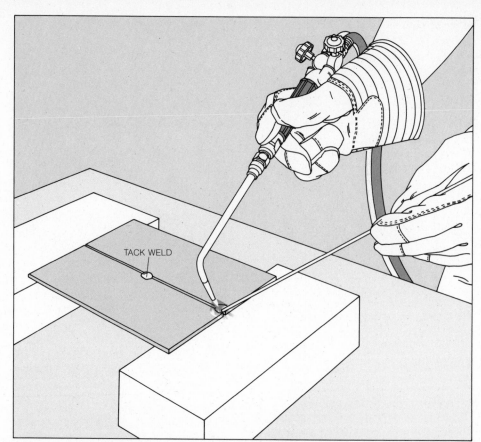

TACK WELD

2 **Closing the joint.** Working from the right edge if you are right-handed and the left edge if you are left-handed, move the puddle along the seam, using the torch to fuse the edges and a filler rod to reinforce the joint. While you work, keep the torch and the rod in the same relative positions as for puddling *(page 77)*.

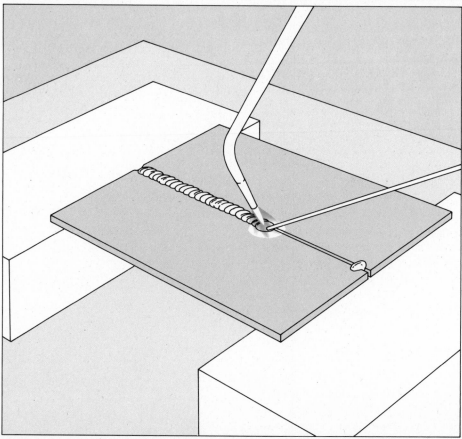

Setting Up and Welding a Lap Joint

1 Preparing the weld. Lay the two pieces of metal to be joined on spaced firebricks, lapping one piece over the other 1 inch. To support the upper piece and keep it level, slip a piece of scrap metal under it, the same thickness as the working stock. Tack-weld the joint, beginning with the center tack. Aim the torch tip at the lower plate, so that the flame will melt both pieces evenly. Tack-weld each end.

2 Sealing the joint. Weld the tacked joint, working from right to left if you are right-handed, left to right if you are left-handed. Use a circular motion on the torch, and direct the flame against the vertical edge so that it catches both pieces of metal. Hold the filler rod against the upper half of the puddle, nearer the top piece of metal, so that the raised band of molten metal is distributed evenly over the two metal surfaces.

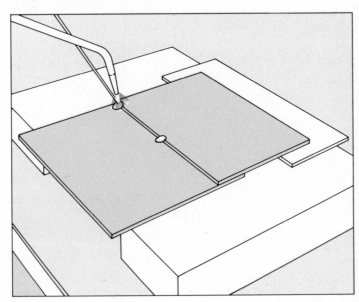

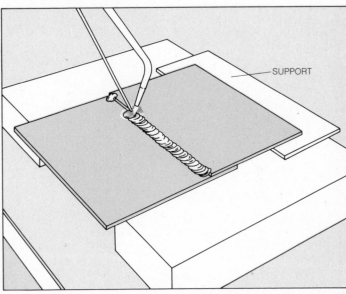

SUPPORT

Welding a T-Shaped Joint

1 Positioning the pieces. Place one piece of metal across two firebrick supports and hold the second piece at right angles to it, grasping the vertical piece with pliers to form a T shape. Aim the lighted torch into one end of the joint, moving it in a circle to form a tack. Then put aside the pliers and use a filler rod to tack the center of the joint, the intermediate tack points and the other end. The first tack, made without filler rod, should be strong enough to steady the vertical piece until the remaining tacks are made.

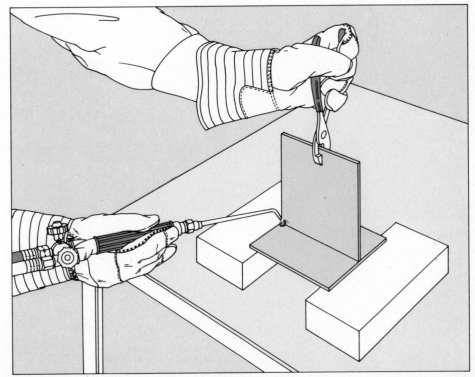

2 Closing the joint. Beginning at the right end if you are right-handed and at the left end if you are left-handed, aim the torch tip at the joint. Hold the torch so that the tip is at a 45° angle to the work, midway between the two pieces of metal. Move the torch and the filler rod along the joint, puddling the metal with circular motions of the torch. Keep the inner cone of the flame about 1/16 inch above the metal surfaces. Hold the tip of the filler rod slightly above the midpoint of the puddle, in the top half of the weld; this will help keep the vertical piece from overheating.

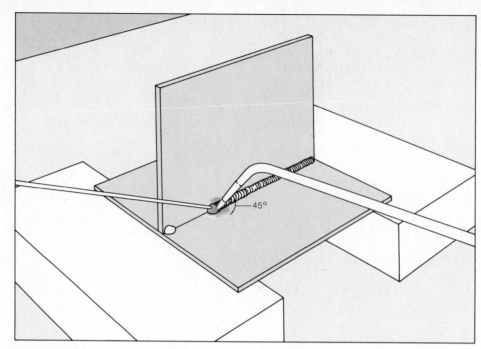

How to Weld an Outside-Corner Joint

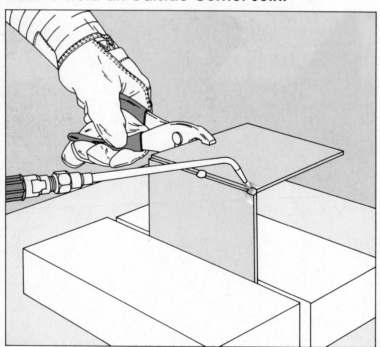

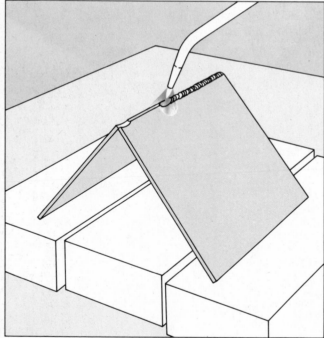

1 Setting up the joint. Wedge one piece of metal vertically between two firebricks; hold the second piece at a right angle to it, grasping the horizontal piece with pliers. Aim the torch at the angle between the two pieces in the middle of the joint, moving the torch in a circle to form a tack. Then tack each end and the intermediate tack points in the same way. You can use a filler rod to strengthen these tacks. When the tacks are done, set the joined pieces across the firebricks to form an inverted V.

2 Fusing the corner closed. Beginning at the right end of the joint if you are right-handed and at the left end if you are left-handed, move the torch in a circular motion across the corner's edge. Hold the torch so that the tip of the flame is split by the edge, keeping the tip of the inner cone 1/16 inch above the edge. When it is completed, the weld ought to fill the angle between the two pieces of metal.

Cutting Metal with a Special Torch Tip

Fitting an oxyacetylene torch with a special cutting attachment converts it into a tool that will cut straight or curved lines, punch small holes and cut out large holes, or slice through pipes and solid metal rods. The cutting attachment is also an ideal tool for beveling the edges of thick pieces of metal that are to be butt-welded.

Before being cut, the metal is preheated to a bright red by a circle of flames produced by the cutting attachment's special tip. After the metal is heated, a lever sends a blast of oxygen through a center hole in the tip to burn away the metal as the torch moves along the cut line. In preheating, the tip of the torch is held about ½ inch above the metal; during cutting, the tip is raised slightly. For accuracy, mark the cut line with a soapstone pencil, whose mark remains visible even when heated. Or mark the line with a center punch *(page 12)*, placing indentations about ¼ inch apart. A metal jig clamped along the line can also be used to guide the torch tip.

As for welding, different tip sizes are available for cutting metals of different thicknesses. A chart for the brand of tip you are using will recommend which size to use, as well as prescribing oxygen and acetylene working pressures, which differ from welding pressures.

Regulating the flame. Set up the rig as for welding *(pages 73-74, Steps 1 to 3)*, and screw the cutting attachment and its tip onto the torch handle. Turn the adjusting screws on the regulators until the working pressures for the oxygen and the acetylene match those recommended for the tip size. To light the torch, open the oxygen valve on the torch handle all the way and the acetylene valve about a half turn, then use a spark lighter at the tip. Adjust the oxygen-control knob on the cutting attachment until the preheat flames are neutral. Press the cutting lever momentarily and check the appearance of the cutting flame; readjust to a neutral flame if necessary, and check to see if a center streak of consistent diameter runs almost the full length of the flame. If the streak is not there, clean out the center hole of the tip.

Anatomy of a cutting attachment. Screwed onto an oxyacetylene-torch handle in place of a welding tip, a cutting attachment feeds a mixture of oxygen and acetylene gas through a single tube to a ring of small holes in the tip *(inset)*; this mixture preheats the metal for cutting. To cut the metal, a separate tube, opened and closed by a cutting lever, carries unmixed oxygen to the large cutting hole in the center of the tip. The oxygen-control knob is used to adjust the flow of oxygen to the preheat holes. The large center hole carries full line pressure.

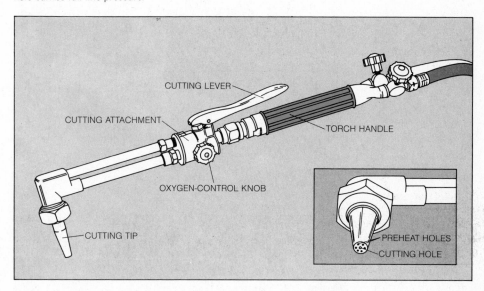

CUTTING LEVER

CUTTING ATTACHMENT

TORCH HANDLE

OXYGEN-CONTROL KNOB

CUTTING TIP

PREHEAT HOLES
CUTTING HOLE

Preparing the Oxyacetylene Rig for Cutting

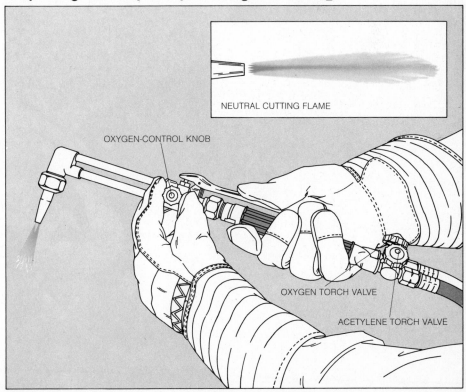

NEUTRAL CUTTING FLAME

OXYGEN-CONTROL KNOB

OXYGEN TORCH VALVE

ACETYLENE TORCH VALVE

Torch-cutting along a Straight Line

Using a homemade jig. Mark a cutting line on the metal with a soapstone pencil or a center punch, and position the workpiece on a metal-topped worktable so that the line clears the edge of the table by at least 5 inches. Using two C clamps, secure a length of angle iron about ¼ inch behind the cutting line, to serve as a jig. Resting the side of the torch against the jig, preheat the metal along the line. You can steady the torch by supporting your forearm on the table. When the metal is bright red, press the oxygen lever gradually and move the cutting flame steadily along the line, guiding the tip with the jig.

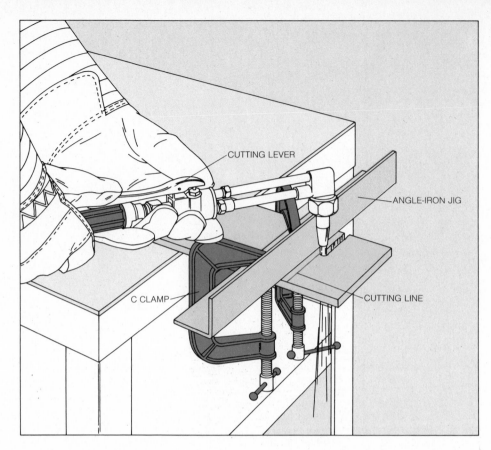

Torch-cutting to Form a Beveled Edge

Beveling with an angle-iron jig. Mark the cutting line, and position the metal on the worktable so that the cutting line clears the edge of the table by about 5 inches. Place a length of angle iron, upside down to form an inverted V, ¼ inch inside the cutting line. To hold the angle-iron jig in place, butt its back leg against the feet of two C clamps. Preheat the metal along the cutting line; when it is bright red, depress the oxygen lever and move the cutting flame steadily along the line. Rest the side of the torch against the sloping face of the jig in order to cut through the metal at a 45° angle.

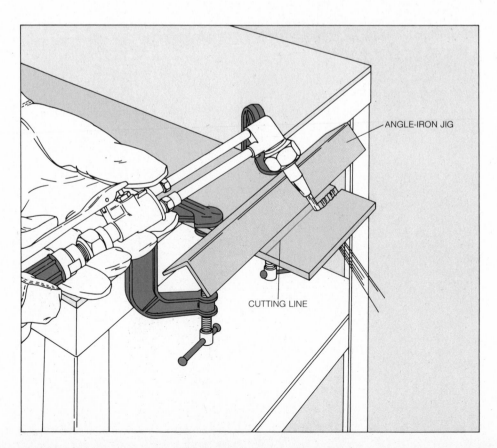

Using the Torch to Cut Holes or Pipes

Cutting large and small holes. For a hole up to ½ inch in diameter, preheat the spot, holding the torch tip about 1/16 inch above the metal surface. Then gradually press the oxygen lever, and raise the tip slightly to pierce the metal. For a larger hole, outline the hole and pierce a hole in the center of the outline. Cut out to the perimeter, then guide the torch along the outline.

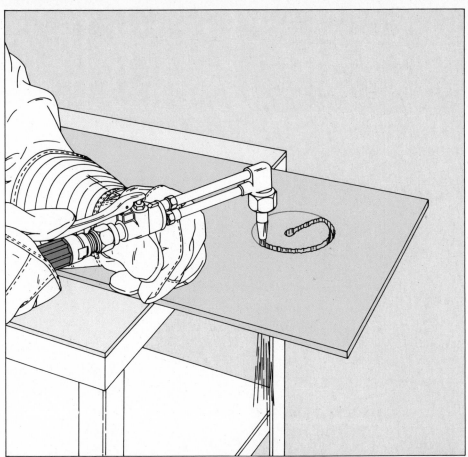

Cutting pipe. Mark a line around the pipe. Beginning at the top of the pipe, aim the torch tip at the pipe center, preheat the metal, then press the oxygen lever to pierce a hole. Keeping the tip always aimed at the pipe center, cut around one side to the midpoint of the bottom. Release the oxygen lever, then lift the torch and, beginning again at the top of the pipe, reheat the pipe and cut down the other side.

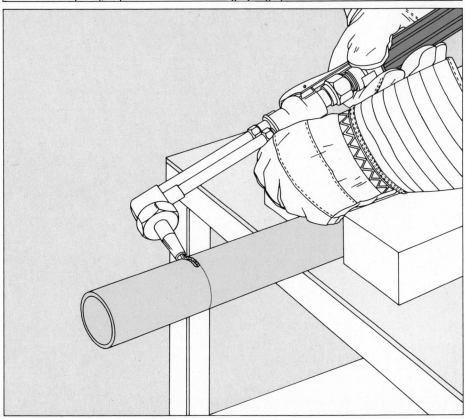

Bending Steel with a Torch

Although soft or thin metals can be bent cold *(pages 20-23)*, thick pieces of steel must be heated to make them malleable. The necessary heat is provided by an oxyacetylene torch fitted with a tip that will distribute the flame evenly over the area that is to be bent. The best tip for the job is a special heating tip called a rosebud, which has six flame-spreading orifices. A standard welding tip that is large enough to weld metal ¼ inch thick will also serve—most manufacturers label it a No. 5 tip. Or you can use a No. 3 or No. 7 tip.

When bending metal with oxyacetylene equipment you must, as when welding, wear a tinted face mask or tinted goggles to protect your eyes from sparks and glare. You will also need insulated welder's gloves and a shop apron or coveralls. Be sure to set up the oxyacetylene equipment in accordance with the instructions and safety precautions noted on pages 72-73.

The bending techniques shown here can be used to make simple, single bends in mild-steel rods up to 4 inches in diameter, flat strips up to 4 inches thick, and standard cap moldings—the stock shaped for stair railings *(page 91)*. Heavier stock or projects requiring composite bends call for special bending machinery, which is usually available only in metalworking shops.

The first step in making any bend is to mark its location with a soapstone pencil. The metal is then clamped in a vise secured to a fireproof work surface.

Many bending jobs require no other tools. If the bend is to be 8 inches or more from the end of the piece of metal, you can make it by heating the stock at the bend point, then pressing down on the end of the metal with your gloved hand. If the bend is closer to the end, you will need to slip a length of pipe over the end as an extender. You can check the angle by means of a combination square set with a protractor head after the metal has cooled, then reheat it and make adjustments. But repeated heating and cooling at the same spot will eventually cause metal fatigue.

When you are bending metal into a curve like the head of a cane—to use at the end of a stair railing, for example—you may have to fabricate a bending tool.

There are few common tools that give you just the right leverage at just the right angle to achieve such a shape.

The bending tool shown in Step 2, page 85, is made of a foot-long piece of stair-railing post stock welded between two pieces of longer channel iron. A piece of bar material, welded to one end, forms a T handle.

Smooth curls in thick metal are made with fixed bending guides, called jigs; these often consist of nothing more than a piece of thick-walled pipe with the same radius as the planned curve. The jig and the metal are clamped in a vise together; once the metal is hot, it is simply wrapped around the jig.

A Simple Straight Bend

1 Heating the metal. With a soapstone pencil, mark a line across the stock to indicate the center of the bend. Clamp the stock in a vise. Light the torch and adjust it to a neutral flame. Play the flame back and forth along the line, keeping it directly on the line to ensure that the bend will be straight.

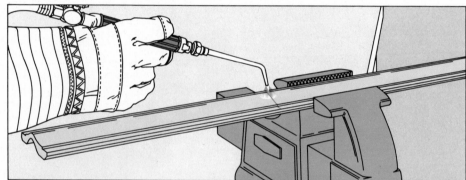

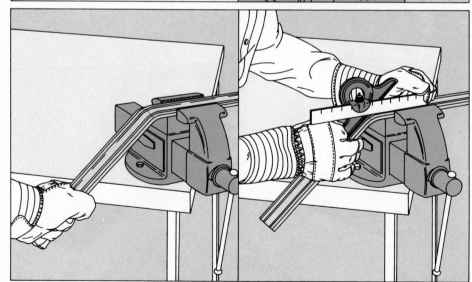

2 Bending the metal. When the area along the line is bright orange, turn off the torch and set it aside. Press straight down with one hand on the end of the metal—applying even, firm pressure—to bend it on the line *(above, left)*. Brush off scale at the bend with a wire brush.

After the metal has cooled enough that it will not damage the tool, hold a combination square set with a protractor head against the workpiece to check the angle of the bend *(above, right)*. If the angle is not right, reheat the metal and adjust the bend.

A Curve to Finish the End of a Railing

1 **Marking and heating the stock.** Mark the metal where the curve will start, clamp the piece in a vise and light the torch, setting it for a neutral flame. Starting at the one end of the line, move the flame across the metal, down one edge, across the end and up the other edge to the line. Repeat this pattern with the torch until the entire section glows bright orange. Turn off the torch and set it aside.

2 **Turning the curve.** With a bending tool, grip the hot metal about ¼ inch from the end and turn it down into a curve *(inset),* using the same motion—on a larger scale—as if you were starting to open a tin can with a key. Sight along the top of the stock to see if the bend is even. If it is not, use the side of the bending tool to pound the metal into line while it is still hot. Brush the scale off the metal with a wire brush.

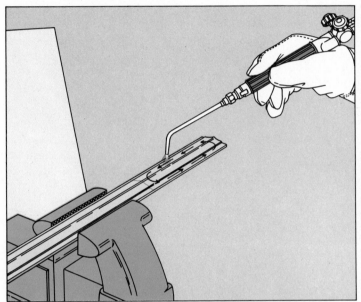

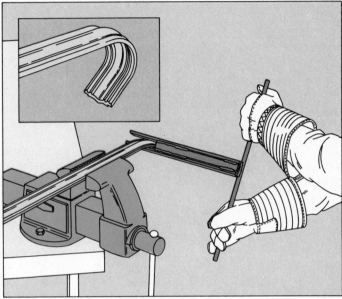

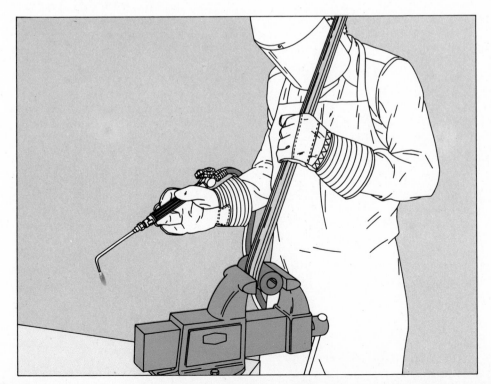

Turning a Curve into an Even Curl

Using a jig. Clamp the metal to be bent beside a length of pipe in a vise, catching the end of the metal between the pipe and the far vise jaw. Heat the section to be bent until it is bright orange. Grip the end of the metal—with your gloved hand if the bend is more than 8 inches away, otherwise with a pipe extender—and steadily pull the metal around the jig. Continue pulling and heating until an even curl results.

Arc Welding: Hot Metal from an Electric Spark

The brilliant blue light and the dramatic fountain of sparks characteristic of arc welding are produced when a strong electric current is forced to jump, or arc, across a short gap in an electrical circuit generated by the welding rig. As the current passes between a metal electrode and the workpiece, air resistance creates temperatures from 7,000 to 10,000° F., melting both the tip of the electrode and a bit of the workpiece into a weld bead as strong as the original metal.

For successful arc welding, you must first learn to apply the right amount of current to the right location for the right amount of time—an action called striking the arc. The arc must then be moved away at a rate that allows the weld to solidify in an even bead that adequately penetrates the work metal.

The intensity of light and heat emitted during welding requires special precautions to protect skin and eyes (box, opposite.) When you buy your arc-welding rig, purchase the necessary safety gear: an arc-welding helmet with a Shade 10 or darker lens, safety glasses with tinted lenses (called flash glasses), gauntlet-style leather or asbestos gloves, and a jacket of leather or treated cotton that will resist hot metal and flying sparks.

Most arc-welding rigs use either alternating current (AC) or direct current (DC), although some rigs can use both. A DC welder can be used with a wider range of electrodes. However, AC units, which operate on 240-volt household current, are the lightest, easiest to use and least costly.

Two other characteristics distinguish the various welding machines on the market. One is their amperage output capacity—the maximum electric current they deliver. The other is their duty cycle, a figure that tells how many minutes out of 10 they can produce that maximum output without overheating. For example, a machine rated for 225 amps at a 60 per cent duty cycle should not be welding at the 225-amp setting for more than 6 minutes out of every 10. For the other 4 minutes, the machine must idle and cool.

Rarely is an arc-welding rig used at top capacity for extended periods of time. For home welding jobs, a 225-amp AC machine with a 20 per cent duty cycle is a good choice. Buy a machine with a continuous amperage setting, which will enable you to fine-tune the arc. The welding-supply store should provide you with an insulated electrode holder, a ground clamp, and cables and connectors to match the amperage rating of your machine.

Take care to locate your welding rig in a place that is well protected against fire. A garage or well-ventilated basement with a cement floor and masonry walls is best. Making a steel welding table (page 11) is useful practice, and such a table is handy for small welding projects. But you can weld on firebricks set on a masonry floor, or you can work outdoors. However, your workplace must have a 240-volt grounded electrical circuit with its own circuit breaker or fuse block.

The last step before striking an arc and beginning to weld is to select the correct electrode for the metal you are working with. Electrodes are metal rods coated with a chemical flux that vaporizes during welding to shield the molten metal from oxygen and nitrogen in the air, which could weaken the weld. Part of the flux also mixes with the weld metal, floating impurities to the top of the weld and forming an insulating coating called slag. The type of flux on an electrode affects how the arc behaves and how deeply the arc melts the workpiece.

All of the hundreds of electrodes available are categorized by the American Welding Society Code. According to this code, an E6013 electrode, for example, is intended for electric-arc welding—as are all electrodes beginning with the letter E. The first two numbers, multiplied by 1,000, indicate the tensile strength of the core metal: 60,000 pounds per square inch (psi) in this case. The third number indicates which of the four basic welding positions—flat, vertical, horizontal, or overhead—the electrode was designed for (1 means all positions; the others are designated 2, for horizontal and flat, or 3, for flat only). The last digit identifies the type of current to use the electrode with: in this case, either AC or DC.

As a general rule, you should buy an electrode that has core metal to match that of your work and a core diameter that matches the thickness of your work—up to 1/8 inch. A 1/8-inch electrode is used with thicker metal, as well: In this case, bevel the edges to be joined, and build up the weld in layers.

For your first welds, practice with E6013 electrodes with a 1/8-inch diameter, joining pieces of 3/16-inch mild-steel plate. Later, experiment with electrodes recommended by your welding-supply dealer for the work you are planning.

Whatever electrode you buy, it should come with specifications for the amperage range to use when you weld with it. The amperage required generally increases with the thickness of the rod but also varies somewhat with the brand and composition of the electrode.

Before starting to weld, clean the workpiece, and square the joint edges with a sander-grinder (page 19) and a file (page 17). Then fasten the ground clamp in place on the work, leveling the work on scrap metal if necessary. Set the amperage in the middle of the range specified for your electrode, and test your technique on scrap metal of the same type and thickness as the work. Adjust the amperage while the machine idles, until you get a satisfactory weld bead.

Safety Guidelines for Arc Welders

☐ Never strike an arc without having the faceplate of your welding helmet down. Do not allow unprotected persons within sight of the arc.

☐ Wear safety glasses, called flash glasses, at all times, both to protect your eyes in case the arc is struck accidentally and to shield them from particles of metal.

☐ Leave no skin exposed to the heat of the arc. Wear heavy gauntlet-style leather or asbestos gloves, and keep your shirt collar buttoned and your sleeves rolled down. Wear dark clothing of leather or of fire-resistant cotton that is free of grease or oil. Never wear synthetic fabrics while you are welding.

☐ Eliminate traps for spattered metal by wearing trousers that do not have cuffs and keeping your pockets buttoned. As a further precaution, wear heavy boots that cover your ankles.

☐ Use tongs or pliers, not your hands, to grasp metal that has been welded: Both the workpiece and the electrode will be extremely hot.

☐ Be certain that your workplace is well ventilated. Use a portable fan for extra ventilation when working on galvanized or zinc-coated steel, which can emit toxic fumes.

☐ Remove all combustible materials from the welding area, and keep a fire extinguisher handy at all times. If a fire should break out, unplug the welding rig before you smother the fire with the extinguisher.

☐ Never weld in a damp area. Keep hands and clothing dry.

☐ Inspect your equipment regularly. Do not use the machine if its electrode holder, its ground clamp or its connectors are loose or if the insulation on any part shows signs of wear.

☐ Disconnect the welder from its power source whenever you leave it unattended and when you are cleaning, inspecting or repairing it.

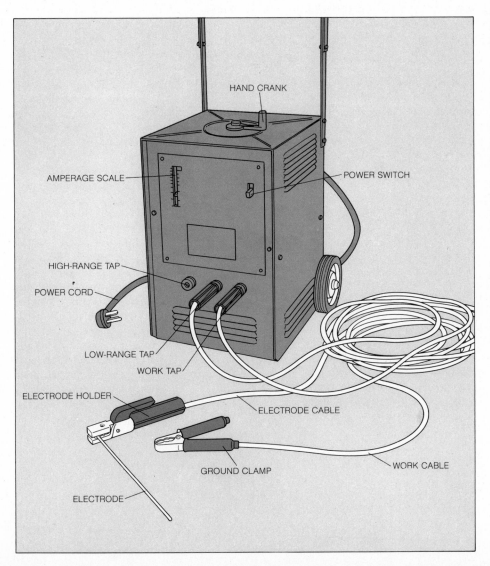

HAND CRANK

AMPERAGE SCALE

POWER SWITCH

HIGH-RANGE TAP

POWER CORD

LOW-RANGE TAP

WORK TAP

ELECTRODE HOLDER

ELECTRODE CABLE

GROUND CLAMP

WORK CABLE

ELECTRODE

Anatomy of a Machine that Heats to 7,000°

Anatomy of an arc-welding rig. When the power cord of this AC welder is plugged into a 240-volt receptacle, a transformer inside reduces the household voltage to roughly 80 volts while increasing the amperage to as high as 230 amperes. Two sockets for the electrode cable—called taps—permit a choice of low or high amperage ranges. Within these two ranges, the hand crank makes finer amperage adjustments, indicated by a scale on the front of the machine. A third socket, the work tap, receives the work cable, which leads to the ground clamp.

In operation, the ground clamp is fastened to the workpiece, the power switch is on, and the electrode in its holder is held just above the workpiece. Current from the transformer flows through the electrode, from which it arcs to the workpiece, heating it to more than 7,000°. The current completes the circuit to the transformer through the ground clamp and work cable.

Mastering the Basic Stringer Bead for Welds

1 **Striking an arc.** With the amperage adjustment set at 115, fasten the ground clamp to a piece of mild-steel scrap, then insert the bare end of the electrode at a 90° angle into the jaws of the electrode holder. Turn on the machine.

Position the tip of the electrode 1 inch above the workpiece, flip down the welder's mask, then move the electrode toward the work with a slight sweeping motion—striking the electrode on the metal as you would strike a long match.

As soon as the arc appears, lift the electrode ⅛ inch above the workpiece, holding it perpendicular to the face of the metal. When a molten puddle appears at the tip, pull the electrode away to break the arc. If the electrode touches the work, it will stick to the metal, but you can usually free it with a quick twisting movement. Sometimes, though, it may be necessary to release the electrode from the holder and knock the electrode free with a chipping hammer.

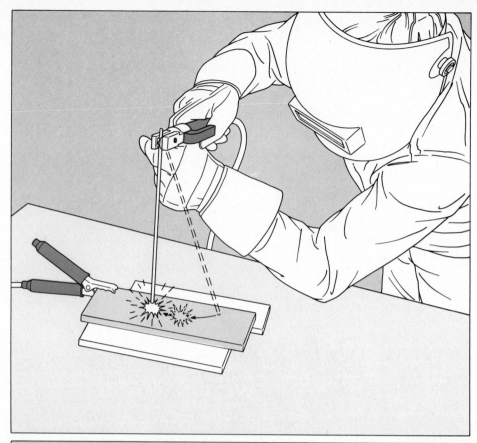

2 **Running a bead.** Strike an arc near one end of a ¼ inch scrap of mild steel. When weld metal begins to build up behind the molten puddle near the tip of the electrode, angle the electrode holder slightly so that the upper end of the electrode tilts about 15° toward the direction of travel, and move the electrode straight across the workpiece at a rate of about 2 inches per minute. Listen to the sound of the arc; when the electrode is the correct distance above the metal and is moving at the correct speed, you will hear a sharp crackling sound like that of bacon frying.

As the electrode is consumed, steadily lower the electrode holder to maintain the arc length at ⅛ inch. If you complete the weld before the electrode is reduced to a 2-inch stub, clean the weld *(opposite, top)*. If you do not finish the weld before reducing the electrode to a stub, replace the electrode with a new one, clean the weld, and resume welding the bead.

To complete an interrupted bead, strike an arc ½ inch beyond the depression at the end of the bead, called the crater *(inset)*. Move the electrode back over the crater to fuse the new weld metal with the old, then reverse direction again, continuing in the original direction.

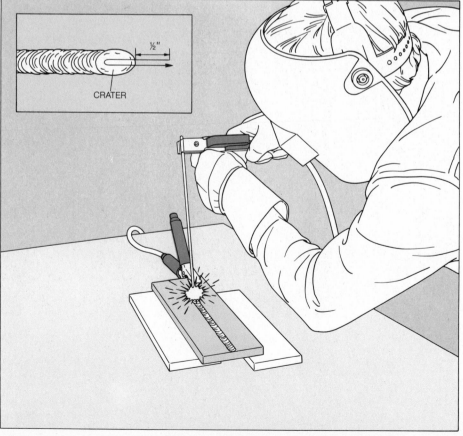

½"

CRATER

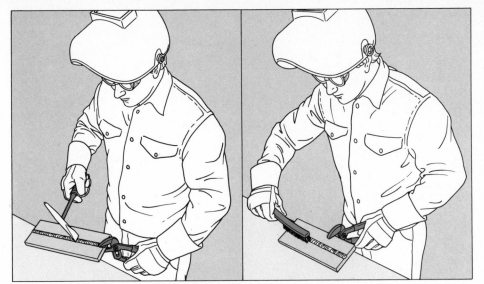

Slag Removal with Hammer and Wire Brush

Removing slag. Hold the hot workpiece steady with pliers or tongs, and loosen the slag that coats the weld bead; strike along the length of the bead with the square end of a chipping hammer *(far left).* Then run the hammer's pointed end along the junction of the weld bead and the workpiece to remove slag.

Finish cleaning the weld with a stiff wire brush *(near left).* Scrub firmly all along the length of the bead, then brush across it to sweep away the last remaining particles of slag.

How to Recognize a Solid Weld Bead

Judging a bead. Seen from above and in cross section, these seven beads show the effects of the three major components of welding technique: current setting, arc length, and electrode speed. The smooth, even ripples in the first example at the left indicate a good bead, with equal amounts of weld metal evident above and below the surface of the work.

Moving toward the right, the next two beads show the effects of incorrect amperage. First, because the current was too low, the bead failed to penetrate. Then, too much current made the weld crater too large and spattered.

In the fourth and fifth beads, the welder misjudged the electrode's distance from the work.

Too short an arc left a superficial bead. Too long an arc made a shallow, spattered bead.

The last two beads at the right illustrate the importance of the rate at which the electrode is moved along the workpiece. Too slow a movement left excessive waste metal, and too much speed created a shallow, elongated bead.

Butt and Fillet Joints— the Two Essential Welds

Tacking a joint. To prevent the heat of the arc from distorting the metal being joined, first fasten the two pieces temporarily with spots of weld metal called tack welds. Locate the tack welds near the ends of the joint, and put additional tack welds at 6-inch intervals at long joints. Strike an arc and hold the tip of the electrode ⅛ inch above the location of the tack for 2 to 4 seconds, depending on the thickness of the metal.

To tack a butt joint in metal ¼ inch of thicker, bevel each edge at a 30° angle; use a bench grinder *(page 19)* or an oxyacetylene torch *(page 82)*. Grind or file the bottom ¹/₁₆ inch of the bevel until it is vertical *(inset),* clean and smooth it, then tack-weld at the base of the groove.

Securing a butt joint. To weld a butt joint in metal less than ¼ inch thick, use the same technique as for a stringer bead *(page 88, bottom),* moving the electrode forward just as it melts the full thickness of both pieces of metal *(inset, top).* Too fast a movement will fail to fuse the joint completely; too slow a movement will burn holes in the joint and leave drips on the back.

To weld a butt joint in metal ¼ inch or thicker, work in layers *(inset, bottom).* Make the first layer—the root pass—with the tip of the electrode almost touching the beveled edges, creating a solid base for the subsequent layers. Clean this weld thoroughly *(page 89),* then deposit additional layers, cleaning after each one, until the weld is ¹/₁₆ inch above the surface of the metal. To cover the full width of the joint with the final layer—the cover pass—make a slight weaving movement with the tip of the electrode.

Making a fillet weld. Holding the electrode so that it bisects the angle of the joint (usually 45° above the base plate), strike an arc, then move the electrode slowly along the seam, slanting it about 20° in the direction of travel. Pace the movement of the electrode so that its tip is always above the leading edge of the molten pool of weld metal. Adjust the amperage setting, if necessary, to produce a triangular weld—its three sides of roughly equal length *(inset, top).* The depth of the weld—called the throat— should equal the thickness of the work metal. If you accidentally undercut the vertical plate *(inset, bottom),* shorten the arc, bring the tip of the electrode slightly closer to the horizontal plate, and move the electrode more slowly.

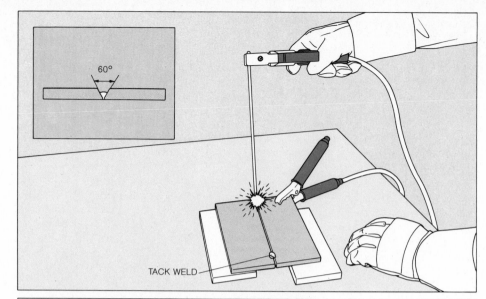

TACK WELD

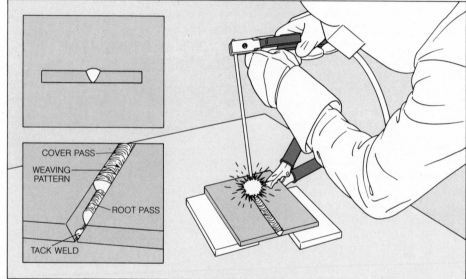

COVER PASS
WEAVING PATTERN
ROOT PASS
TACK WELD

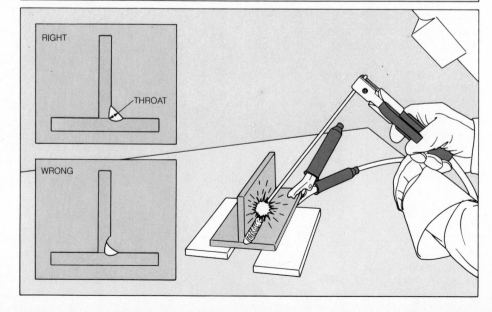

RIGHT
THROAT
WRONG

Fabricating a Steel Stair Rail

Most steel railings are made of vertical bars welded to a frame of crosspieces and posts. The crosspieces may form a parallelogram following the angle of a stairway, or form a rectangle along the edge of a porch. This frame is often topped with an ornamental strip of molded cap rail. To make a long railing, a series of posts may join several frames.

Whatever the configuration of a railing, the bars usually are solid steel ½ inch square. Posts may be made of 11-gauge steel tubing 1 inch square or—for extra strength—of solid steel 1 inch square. Traditionally, the crosspieces are made of 1-inch channel iron punched with square holes for the bars, and the molded cap rail is welded onto the top channel. However, you can save time and money by using a cap rail with the top channel molded into it. Flanges parallel to the edges of the cap rail anchor the bars in place for welding.

Before making a railing for either a stairway or a porch, check the building-code requirements for your area. Use these as the basis for planning the railing and ordering materials.

When you order materials, ask the supplier to cut the steel to length. The cap rail should equal the length of the railing, plus 5 inches for each decorative curve at the ends (page 85)—6 inches if the curve is at the bottom of a stair railing. For a railing like the one shown at right, determine the length (excluding the curves) by measuring from the edge of the top step to the edge of the bottom step and adding 2 inches for the two posts. Use this figure for the channel as well, then make adjustments during construction.

To find the height of the bars, add ½ inch to the distance from the lower channel to the bottom step, and subtract this sum from the railing height; the location of the lower channel and the height of the railing are usually set by code. The length of the posts will depend on how they will be anchored to the stair or porch. If they are to be set into holes drilled in concrete, they should equal the railing height plus 4 inches. However, if the porch or stairway is concrete covered with a brick veneer, add 3 more inches to allow the post to pass through the veneer and into the concrete below. If the porch

or stairway is of concrete shallower than 4 inches, order posts that equal the height of the railing, and anchor them with post flanges and lag bolts.

Ask the steel supplier to prepunch the channel to hold the bars; an interval of 6 inches, center to center, will satisfy most building codes. For a diagonal railing, the holes must be slightly rectangular—½ inch wide and ⅝ inch long. If the supplier cannot prepunch and shear the steel, cut it yourself with a hacksaw, then drill and file the holes.

Once the materials are at hand, a full-scale template for the railing should be drafted on a 4-by-8-foot sheet of ½ inch plywood. Because one edge of the plywood will serve as a reference for all the measurements, that edge must be smooth and the corners square.

To make the butt welds and fillet welds that hold the railing together, you will also need a supply of E6013 electrodes ⅛ inch in diameter. Once the welds are made, grind the butt welds smooth (page 19), coat the railing with rustproof primer, and finish it with black exterior enamel made for metal surfaces.

A steel stair railing. Providing a sturdy handhold on a short flight of steps, this stair railing consists of vertical bars welded at the bottom to a section of U-shaped channel (inset, bottom) and at the top to a molded cap rail (inset, top). The bars fit into holes precut in the channel and between flanges under the cap rail. The flanges on both the channel and the cap rail conceal the welds. Bends in the cap rail and the channel, and curves at both ends of the cap rail, are made with an oxyacetylene welding torch (pages 84-85) before other construction begins.

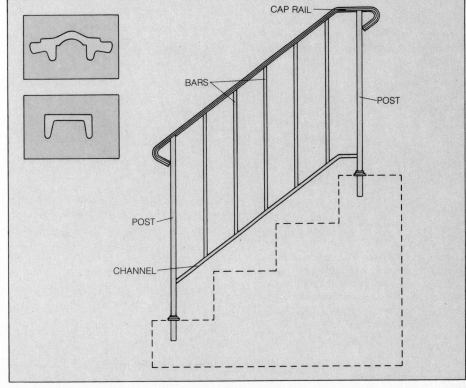

Laying out a Template to Establish Angles Needed

1 Measuring the steps. Four dimensions are critical in plotting a railing for steps. First measure the diagonal length of the stairway from the edge of the top step (or the edge of the porch or stoop) to the edge of the bottom step *(near right)*. Then measure the dimensions of a step: its horizontal depth, called the run, and its height, called the rise. Mark the post angle—the angle between the posts and the stairway slope—on a pitch gauge *(far right)*, a small plywood rectangle. To do this, set one edge of the piece of plywood across the edges of three steps, then hold a level vertically against the board and mark a post line along the edge of the level.

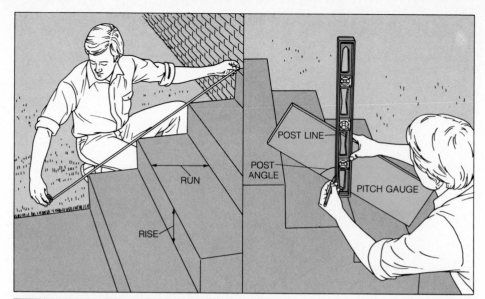

2 Outlining the steps. Using a 4-by-8 sheet of plywood as a template, make two marks on the near edge, spacing the marks to match the stairway's diagonal length. From each mark draw a 16-inch line, using a framing square to make the line perpendicular to the template's edge.

Set the angle of the framing square on the first guideline, with the long arm of the square to your left. Locate the measurement for the run (depth) of the step on the outer edge of the long arm; find the rise (height) on the outer edge of the short arm. With both numbers touching the edge of the template and the apex of the square resting on the guideline, mark along the square's outer edges. Repeat the procedure on the other guideline. Finally, mark the locations of a post on the run of each step, 4 inches from the step's edge *(inset)*.

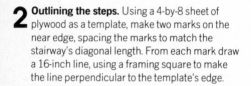

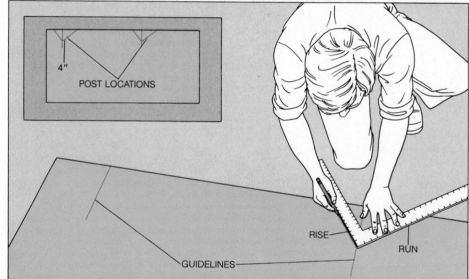

3 Plotting the posts. Using a folding rule, duplicate the post angle on the pitch gauge by setting a short section of the rule against the bottom of the gauge and aligning the longer section with the post line. Then transfer this angle to the template by setting the rule on the template so that the long section intersects the step at a post location. Mark the template along the rule at two points, and repeat at the other post location. Using a straightedge, join the marks and extend these post lines 36 inches above each step.

Measure along both post lines, and mark the height of the bottom channel (usually 6 inches above the run of the step) and the height of the handrail (usually 34 inches above the run of the step). Draw horizontal lines between the post lines to show the locations of the lower channel and the handrail *(inset)*.

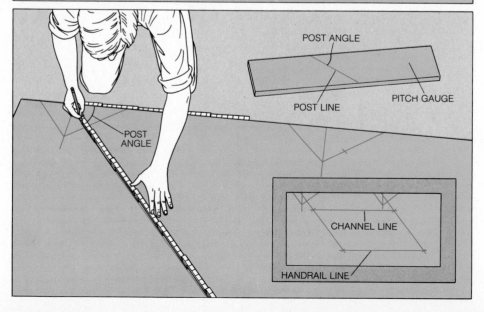

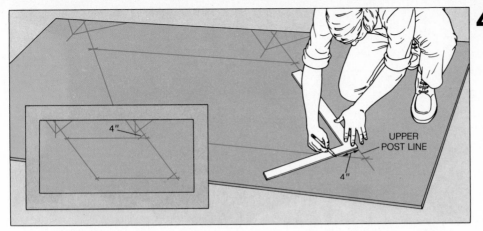

4 **Locating the bend points.** Set the long arm of a framing square along the line for the upper post so that the short arm crosses the line for the handrail. Slide the long arm along the post line until the 4-inch mark on the outer edge of the short arm intersects the handrail line, and trace along the outside edge of the square from the post line to the handrail line. Repeat the procedure near the base of the post line, joining the post line to the line for the channel *(inset)*.

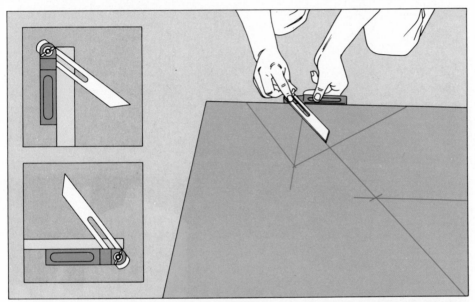

Preparation of the Parts

Beveling post and channel. To measure the angle for the top end of the lower post, set a T bevel on the template where the bottom end of the lower post line meets the template edge. Transfer this angle to the top end of the lower post, setting the handle of the T bevel along the edge of the post so that the angle between handle and blade falls on the post's corner *(inset, top)*. Mark the metal with a soapstone pencil.

Mark the same angle on the end of the bottom channel that abuts the lower post, placing the T bevel's handle along the bottom edge of the channel *(inset, bottom)*. To bevel the stock, clamp it in a vise, fasten a metal straightedge along the cutting line with a C clamp, and cut along the straightedge with a hacksaw *(page 14)*. File away any burrs or rough spots *(page 17)*.

Preparing channel and cap rail. Mark bar locations on the channel with *Xs,* then drill $9/16$-inch holes on these marks *(page 26)*. Secure the channel in a vise, and square the holes with a tapered square file.

Mark the cap rail for notching and bending, using the template as a guide. Mark the lower post location on the rail flanges with two marks 1 inch apart, making the first mark 6 inches from one end of the rail. On the template, measure from the lower post line to the bend in the rail; subtract ½-inch, then mark this distance on the cap rail. Then make two marks for the upper post, 4 inches from the bend line. Cut away the cap-rail flanges at the post locations *(inset)*, using a portable grinder *(pages 18-19)*. If you do not have a portable grinder, omit the slots and fasten the posts to the flanges with fillet welds.

Curve the ends of the cap rail as shown on page 85. Bend the rail with an oxyacetylene torch *(page 84)* to match the angle on the template. Then mark and bend the channel.

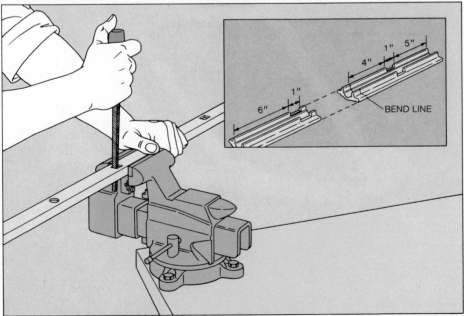

Assembling the Frame and Adding the Bars

1 Welding the framework. Lay the posts, channel, and cap rail in their positions on the template. To transfer the position for the bars from the channel to the cap rail, slide the channel up against the cap rail and mark through the holes in the channel onto the cap rail. Then lay the channel back in position. With the arc welder set for 100 amps, butt-weld both ends of the channel to the posts, adjusting the current, if necessary, to make a good weld bead *(page 89).*

Prop up the channel and posts on scrap metal so that the ends of the posts butt squarely against the cap rail, then butt-weld the upper edges of the posts to the cap-rail flange. Make fillet welds at the tops of the posts. Turn the frame over, and weld along the opposite sides of channel, posts and cap rail.

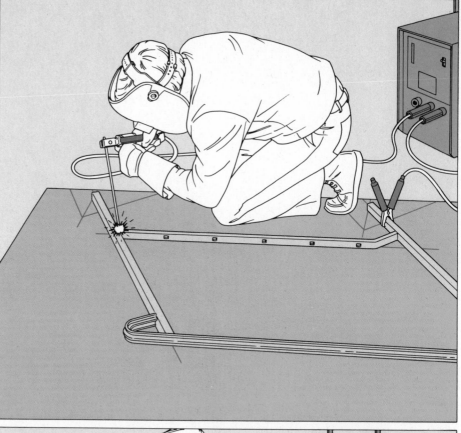

2 Welding the bars. Have a helper hold the framework steady, upside down on the cap rail. Insert the bars one at a time through the holes in the channel, holding each bar on its mark on the cap rail with one hand while, with the other, you make a fillet weld at the end of the bar between the flanges of the cap rail. Then make fillet welds along the sides of the posts between the flanges of the cap rail. Weld the other ends of the bars to the channel with fillet welds inside the channel flanges, then make fillet welds at the junctions of the channel and the posts. Clean all the welds *(page 89).* Turn the railing right side up, and check its alignment. Align the curves with the posts, if necessary, by bending them cold with a homemade bending tool *(page 85).*

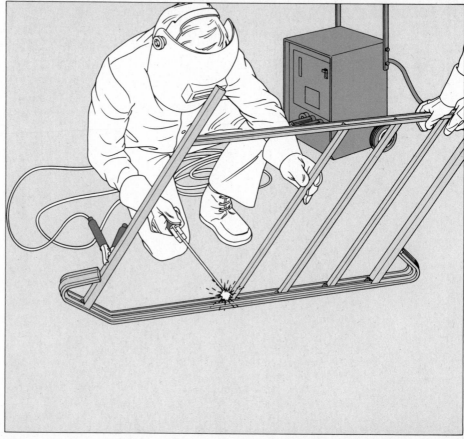

The Final Step: Installation of the Stair Railing

Attaching a railing to a wall. To fasten the horizontal end of a railing to a wall, make a mounting clip by drilling a hole in one leg of an angle iron 1 inch wide *(page 26)*, or use an ornamental mounting clip *(inset)*. While a helper steadies the railing upside down on its cap rail, resting on firebricks, clamp the mounting clip to the underside of the railing with a C clamp, then butt-weld the clip to the cap rail along the edges of the angle iron.

To fasten the railing to a masonry wall, use a lag bolt and an expansion anchor, setting the anchor in a hole drilled with a carbide-tipped masonry bit that matches the anchor's diameter.

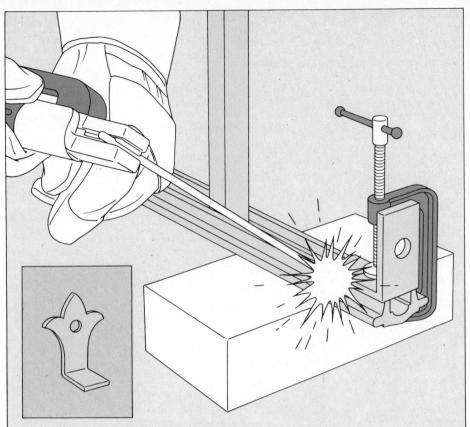

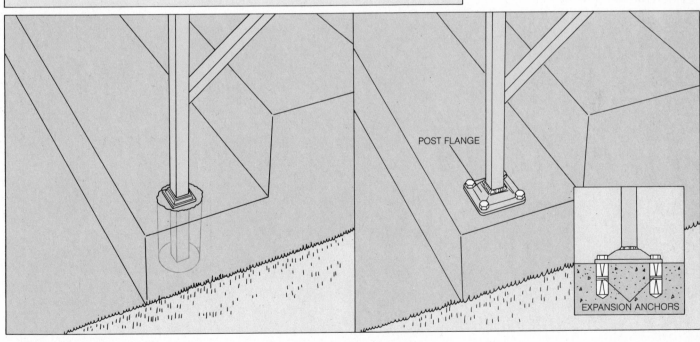

POST FLANGE

EXPANSION ANCHORS

Anchoring the posts. To anchor a railing in concrete *(above, left)*, drill 2-inch postholes 4 inches deep; center each hole 4 inches from the edge of the steps. Use a hammer drill with a carbide-tipped core bit, available from rental agencies. Set the posts in the holes and plumb the railing, bracing it with 2-by-4s or metal bars; fill the holes with anchoring cement.

For a stairway of concrete veneer *(above, right)*, fasten a post flange onto the end of each post with fillet welds. Then fasten the post flanges to the stairway with lag bolts and expansion anchors set into holes in the concrete *(inset)*. Drill these holes with a carbide-tipped masonry bit, making the size of the holes match the outside diameter of the expansion anchors.

Spirited Metal Comes Home

Despite the demonstrated virtues of metal building materials in office buildings, factories, schools and hospitals, such items as steel I beams and anodized-aluminum panels have never gained wide acceptance in home construction. People wedded to such traditional materials as wood, plaster, brick and stone have resisted these unconventional substitutes, presuming them to be too cold and too crude for domestic comfort. Yet, as the pictures in the following portfolio demonstrate, metal building materials—used with imagination and a fine sense of design—can produce pleasurable and even elegant living quarters.

The art in using these materials successfully is to accept them for what they are, rather than trying to make them seem something else. Metal framing—to take the most fundamental example—offers engineering advantages over wood. Pound for pound and girth for girth, iron and steel columns and girders are several times stronger than wooden posts and beams. Walls consequently can be lighter and spans can run unsupported for substantially greater lengths.

The benefits of such framing are many. A designer can increase the amount of glass in exterior walls, for instance, and can safely provide much more column-free, wall-free interior space. In addition, metal framing opens the possibility of using what architects call systems building—the creation of an entire house from standardized modular parts. Depending on the module chosen, the designer can use a closed system, employing only the components of a single manufacturer, or an open system, in which components from many sources are mixed.

Quite apart from such practical considerations, metal framing, when left open to view, can also be pleasing to the eye. Its articulated parts, often cleanly engineered and cleverly joined, are as fascinating to look at as the exposed works of a ticking clock.

Other metal building materials offer similar design features. Factory-made exterior paneling of steel and aluminum, for example, is lightweight, easy to install and often available with a finish that requires minimum maintenance. Some versions are factory-primed, ready to paint; others are anodized or permanently coated with colorful factory-hardened enamel. One of the most intriguing paneling materials is a copper-bearing steel that weathers to a deep, rich brown and stays that way, year in and year out.

Designers can also draw upon an almost limitless catalogue of nonstructural metal components—iron stairs and railings like those of ships; embossed-steel safety flooring designed for factories; pressed-metal ceiling panels and satin-surfaced wall panels; skylights and track lighting; modular storage systems invented for warehouse operations; and the stainless-steel plumbing and cabinetry made for professional kitchens.

Situated in residential settings and played off against more conventional materials and furnishings, these components can introduce a note of dramatic tension, unexpected humor and, quite often, a sense of classic good taste. And the wonder of it is—as one designer pointed out—that the potential has been there all along, "right under our noses." Ever since the days of cast-iron sheathing on office buildings and the soaring arches of Victorian railroad stations, it has been clear that metal can be beautiful.

Flying buttresses. Massive iron girders, joined in a truss configuration reminiscent of traditional Gothic buttressing, carry their heavy responsibility with panache. The supports were installed during a major renovation of the 18th Century Venetian palace, in which several old wooden beams and the original ceiling were removed. Rather than trying to camouflage the reinforcements, the architect chose to paint them an attention-getting antirust red.

Ruggedly Handsome Structural Steel

Metal skeletons were a liberating force in 19th Century industrial architecture, making possible tall buildings, the extensive use of glass, and the vast interior spaces that marked the metropolitan railroad terminal in its heyday *(right)*. But it has taken a desire for open living space to make iron and steel structural members welcome in the home.

On these pages, three contemporary designs demonstrate practical but visually rich uses for architectural metalwork in domestic settings. In the examples opposite, novel adaptations modify existing structures; the home below shows what can be done when the designer starts from scratch, creating a dramatic living space from standardized factory parts.

High and mighty landmark. This 1906 classic, New York's now-demolished Pennsylvania Railroad Station, used the structural vocabulary of factory and conservatory in its soaring spaces. Iron and steel armatures supported acres of glass in walls, domes and roof arches.

Flying deck. To make maximum use of a 20-foot-high nave while preserving the architectural integrity of this converted 19th Century chapel, a small, airy mezzanine was built at one end. Iron stairs lead up to an industrial grillwork floor that filters light into the area below.

Bare-bones treatment. Vivid reminders of the time when this London waterfront flat was a tea warehouse are these rows of splayed steel posts. The four shown here define the fireplace seating area; other posts set off the sleeping area in the master bedroom.

Foursquare and flexible. Modular steel framing establishes the plan of the interior at left, and such off-the-rack industrial parts as metal panels, doors and stairs, and metal-framed windows define the living spaces. This is one of two households, each with the same internal framing system, that share a larger structure.

Armored Exteriors: Clad for a Long and Carefree Life

Metal has been used as an exterior facing material for industrial buildings since the mid-19th Century, when cast-iron façades like the one at the left decorated urban thoroughfares all over America.

Made originally in the image of more costly carved stone, exterior metal paneling has since gone through many transformations, in terms of fabrication techniques, materials and applications. Today's choices range from aluminum siding that imitates wood clapboards to a wide range of less-orthodox designs, including those shown here. They all offer potential economies in that they can be coordinated with modular framing systems, their preformed parts going up on the site with little waste and a minimum of hand labor.

Bridge over tranquil waters. Because the structure at right hovers on pylons over a pond, lightweight water-resistant materials were chosen. Exterior wall panels, fixed to a steel frame, are of copper-bearing steel. The rich brown tone is the result of oxide formation.

Skin-deep beauty. Faced with interlocking panels of cast iron, New York's Haughwout Building of 1857 is a justly celebrated example of the once-common practice of dressing up plain-Jane commercial structures with lavishly wrought exteriors. Here the successful disguise is a factory-made version of a Venetian palace.

Clarity of purpose. Corrugated aluminum, a more durable version of late-1940s barn roofing, demarcates sleeping and service areas of this Vermont home. Expressive of the material's malleable nature, corners—including those of the windows—are rounded, forming a counterpoint to the angular forms of the house itself.

Fun house. As in a child's toy, prefabricated aluminum panels are visibly bolted to the framework of this hillside house with a cantilevered deck.

Shimmering Accents for Texture and Design

Since the time of high Victorian architecture, the potential decorative uses of metal have been limited only by the imagination of individual designers. As a ceiling covering, for example, pressed sheet steel painted white can do a creditable job of imitating fancy plasterwork. But installed in an untraditional fashion, as in the room at right, it takes on an unconventional and thoroughly contemporary sleekness.

Similarly, satin-finish metals can be used to play tricks with light and space. And if the intended look is spare and the renovation minimal, nothing delivers more drama for less money than a wall-wide factory shelving system.

All that glitters. The stainless-steel walls of this rehabilitated New York eatery were the ultimate in 1930 diner design. Quilted in a fan pattern that multiplied the metal's own dazzle, the panels also aided harried countermen: The irregular surfaces stayed clean-looking longer.

Space technology. To enlarge the visual dimensions of this narrow dining room, the walls have been wrapped in light-reflecting satin-finished aluminum sheets. The ceiling, similarly clad, is dropped several inches below the original, to achieve more pleasing proportions and to make wells for round aluminum spotlights.

Tin ceiling recast. To demarcate the informal boundaries of this apartment dining area, sheets of traditionally patterned pressed metal have been nailed over a wood frame and suspended from the ceiling. Painted an appetizing raspberry red, they also serve as a reflecting canopy for a glass-shaded industrial lamp, casting a rosy glow over the diners.

Reflected glory. Distant cousin to an oldtime diner, this narrow kitchen sparkles beneath a corrugated-aluminum ceiling. The material does an effective job of spreading ambient light but, equally important to the designer, it matches the corrugated exterior siding *(page 100)*, adding to the architectural unity.

Braced for strength. In a converted loft, a prefabricated shelving and storage system organizes a living room carved from open space. Ten feet high and based on an eight-foot span, the system has cross bracing that provides a handsome pattern and tames the 70-foot wall.

Homage to the past. A hefty drive wheel, part of a hoist that once lifted vegetables and boxes to this third-story loft, has been retained as wall sculpture.

Creating Superalloys for the Space Age

Streaking through the sky at high altitude, a jet plane sucks huge amounts of frigid air into its engines. But the inside of each engine is an inferno; there, jet fuel mixed with the air burns at a temperature of 2,500° F., heating the metal of the combustion chamber until it glows bright red. Behind the combustion chamber, turbines whirl in an explosive blast of exhaust gases that heats the turbine blades to about 1,700°.

Such extreme heat is enough to melt or weaken most metals. The critical parts of a modern jet engine, however, are made of remarkable combinations called superalloys, which withstand high heat with undiminished strength, providing long-term reliability.

Since antiquity, metals have been melted together to form alloys—blends that possess properties distinct from those of the constituent metals. Lead-and-tin solder, steel plate and aluminum extrusions are all alloys. Superalloys, based on nickel or cobalt mixed with small amounts of up to a dozen other metals, were developed especially to endure high working temperatures.

The first superalloy, called Nimonic, was created in 1941 by the Mond Nickel Company of Great Britain for use in jet engines, then being developed for combat aircraft. Engineers had tried to make jet-engine turbines from steel alloys—the most advanced structural alloys of their day—but these materials tended to melt at temperatures exceeding 2,000°. Nimonic, as its principal virtue, contained no steel at all. It was a combination of nickel, chromium and titanium and had exceptional strength at high temperatures. With this advance, jet technology—and the development of other superalloys—took off.

There are now hundreds of nickel-based superalloys, with fanciful names like Astroloy and Waspaloy. They contain such exotic metals as tungsten, columbium and molybdenum, in blends that give each a unique combination of heat resistance, corrosion resistance and strength. A new superalloy can be created by a very slight change in the proportion of some of the additives—as little as one tenth of one per cent. As superalloys have proliferated, so have their applications: Among other roles, they are used in corrosion-proof containers for acids, parts for petrochemical plants, and marine equipment.

Spurred by a burgeoning demand for light, strong structural materials, metallurgists have moved beyond superalloys to explore the potential applications of other rare metals. An intensive research effort transformed titanium—dubbed the "wonder metal" in the 1950s for its combination of strength, lightness and heat resistance—from a laboratory curiosity into an important structural alloy. Titanium is now commonly used in the compressors of jet engines, the wings of high-speed aircraft and—on a less exalted transportation front—in the frames of racing bicycles. Anyone can buy sheets, plates and rods of titanium alloy from a metal-products dealer, though its cost is still prohibitive for most uses in the home.

Looking forward to the needs of the space age, metallurgists are investigating the possibilities of using tungsten, columbium, tantalum and other metals with melting points higher than 3,400° as structural alloys. The tendency of these metals to break down in the presence of oxygen limits their application on earth, but in the airless void of space their potential is virtually limitless.

Metals made for space travel. Pictured in orbit 100 miles above the earth, the National Aeronautics and Space Administration's Space Shuttle launches a satellite. The fuselage is made of high-strength aluminum alloys, and the satellite and its rocket engine are sheathed in aluminum and titanium. Many internal parts are nickel-based superalloys.

Molten Metal Cast in a Mold of Moist Sand

Metal casting—the process of shaping metal by melting it and pouring it into a mold—is an ancient craft that has retained its own unique vocabulary and esoteric tools. Items as diverse as wedding rings and engine blocks are cast in metals ranging from gold to aluminum.

There are several techniques for metal casting, varying in expense and in the accuracy and smoothness of the finished casting. In sand casting, a technique used in industry as well as by hobbyists, moist sand is packed around a pattern of the same shape and size as the object to be cast. The pattern is then removed, leaving a casting cavity, and molten metal is poured into the cavity, hardening in the shape of the pattern. The pattern and the sand can be reused any number of times, though a new sand mold must be formed around the pattern each time.

The sand used in sand casting is a special mixture of sand and clay, sometimes called green sand. It must be tempered,

or moistened, with water, and mulled, or mixed, thoroughly before it is used. When squeezed in the hand, sand with the proper moisture content for molding will form a solid lump; when broken in two, the lump will divide cleanly, without crumbling. Some types of molding sand are intended to be moistened with oil instead of water. They have the advantage of not drying out, but they are dirtier and have an unpleasant odor.

Just as important as the molding sand is the pattern used to form the casting cavity. Ready-made patterns for various designs, as well as numbers and letters for personalized plaques, are available from metalworking dealers. But you can also copy existing objects, provided they adapt to the casting process.

Patterns should be of varnished wood or of metal and may consist of one piece or two. A split pattern is joined along the middle by tiny alignment pins before the top of the sand container is placed on

the bottom. A pattern may also have holes for the draw pins that are used to lift the pattern from the sand. All the edges of the pattern pieces must taper slightly. This taper, or draft, lets you remove the pattern from the sand without crumbling the edges of the cavity.

A pattern can also be carved out of polystyrene foam. Such a pattern can be of any shape or complexity, because it does not have to be withdrawn from the mold before the metal is poured. The molten metal simply vaporizes the foam, allowing the metal to replace it. Two disadvantages of this method are that the foam pattern can be used only once (it is destroyed when the metal is poured), and that it cannot be used in an oil-based sand mold because the oil does not permit the vaporized-foam gases to escape. In addition, the vaporizing foam produces noxious fumes. If you are using a polystyrene-foam pattern, be sure to work in a well-ventilated area.

Equipment for making a sand mold. A two-part frame, called the flask, holds the sand in which the mold is formed; it can be of steel, aluminum or wood. The bottom half of the flask is called the drag; the top half, the cope. Two portable platforms—a molding board and a bottom board—are used with the flask as temporary work surfaces. A cloth bag holds the talc-like parting compound that is sprinkled over the pattern and the two adjoining surfaces—or parting planes—of the mold, making them easier to separate. Sand is sifted over the pattern through a wood-framed riddle and is tamped down with a wooden bench rammer. A metal strike-off bar is used for smoothing and leveling the surface of the sand.

A water-filled molder's bulb is used to moisten the edge of the pattern, making it easier to lift from the mold, and draw pins screw into pre-drilled holes in the back of the pattern to facilitate the pattern's removal. A bellows, along with small molding tools such as a trowel and a slick, are used to clean and repair small flaws in the molded-sand impression.

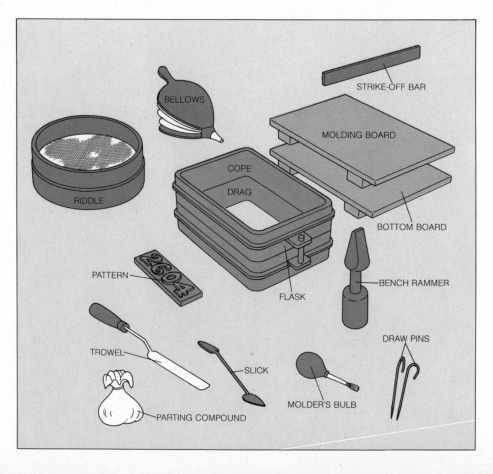

BELLOWS

STRIKE-OFF BAR

MOLDING BOARD

COPE

DRAG

RIDDLE

BOTTOM BOARD

PATTERN

BENCH RAMMER

FLASK

TROWEL

SLICK

DRAW PINS

MOLDER'S BULB

PARTING COMPOUND

A Sand Mold Held by Frames

1 Positioning the pattern. Place the drag upside down on the molding board and center the pattern in the drag, flat side down. Leave enough room between the pattern and the drag for the openings of the riser and the sprue—the passageways through which the molten metal will flow *(page 109, Step 7)*. Dust parting compound evenly over the pattern.

2 Riddling sand over the pattern. Shovel molding sand into a riddle, and sift the sand over the pattern either by shaking the riddle or by pushing the sand through it with your hand. Cover the pattern with sand about 1 inch deep. Then set the riddle aside and use your fingers to tuck the sand around the pattern, working from the sides of the drag in toward the center.

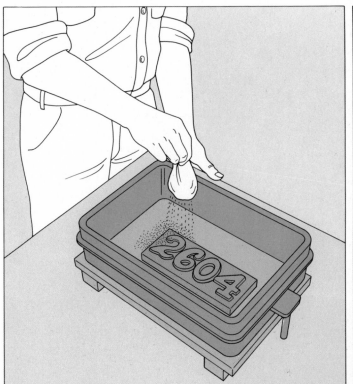

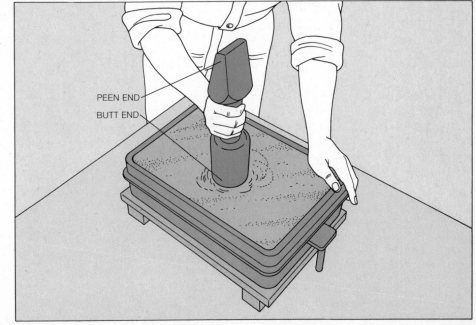

PEEN END

BUTT END

3 Ramming the sand. Shovel more sand into the drag until it is almost full, and compress the sand with a bench rammer. Starting with the peen end of the rammer, push the sand against the sides of the drag, then use the butt end to flatten the sand in the center. Pack the sand firmly, but not so rock-hard that hot gases cannot escape. Load more sand into the drag; ram again, repeating until the level of sand in the drag is slightly higher than the sides of the drag.

4 **Leveling the sand in the drag.** Pull a strike-off bar across the top of the sand, using the edges of the drag as a guide. Work the bar back and forth to make the surface of the sand perfectly flat. Then place the bottom board over the drag, sandwiching the first half of the mold between the bottom board and the molding board.

5 **Rolling the drag.** To turn the drag right side up, grasp the edges of the molding board and the bottom board tightly on each side and flip the drag over. If the drag is especially large or heavy, pull it toward you and roll it over to the opposite side, using the edge of the workbench for leverage. Remove the molding board from the top of the drag, exposing the mold's parting plane and the underside of the pattern.

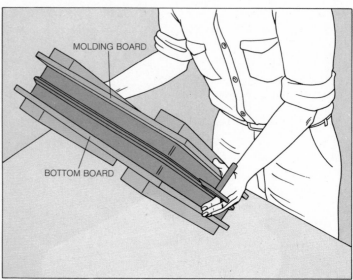

MOLDING BOARD

BOTTOM BOARD

6 **Perfecting the parting plane.** Blow away stray bits of sand with a bellows, and use a trowel or a slick to smooth rough spots or fill in loose areas, especially around the pattern edge. Sprinkle the entire surface lightly with parting compound. For guidance in placing the sprue and the riser *(Step 7)*, measure the distance from the pattern edges to the sides of the drag.

Place the cope on top of the drag, fitting the pins of the drag through the holes of the cope *(inset)*. Sprinkle parting compound over the pattern back, then repeat Steps 2, 3 and 4 to fill the cope.

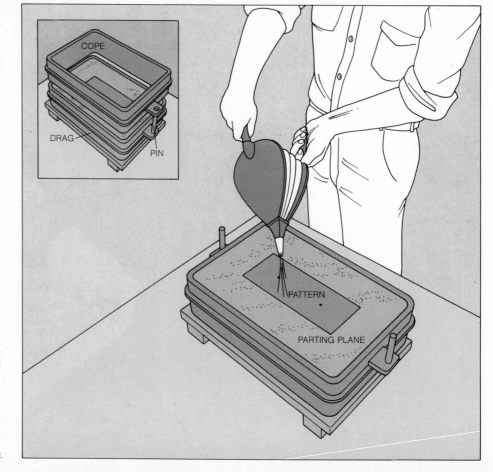

COPE

DRAG

PIN

PATTERN

PARTING PLANE

7 **Cutting the sprue and the riser.** To form the sprue—a passage through which the metal will be poured—measure the depth of the cope, and mark this distance with tape on the side of a section of thin-walled ¾-inch pipe. Push the pipe straight down into the sand in the cope, in a spot where it will not hit the pattern. Twist the pipe back and forth to cut an opening through the sand, stopping when the tape mark meets the surface of the sand. Use a slick to carve a funnel shape in the sand around the pipe, beveling the edges of the sprue opening. Then slip the pipe out, with the sand core inside, leaving a passageway through which to pour the molten metal.

On the other side of the pattern, form the riser opening—the passage into which excess metal will rise—by using a slightly larger diameter pipe to cut through the sand in the cope.

8 **Venting the mold.** Use a $\frac{1}{16}$-inch welding rod or a stiff wire (a bicycle spoke is ideal) to poke channels through the sand in the cope, so that hot gases can escape. Push the rod into the sand, stopping about ½ inch from the pattern. Make about a dozen vents over the pattern area.

Lift the cope from the drag and set it on edge, off to one side, where it will not be disturbed.

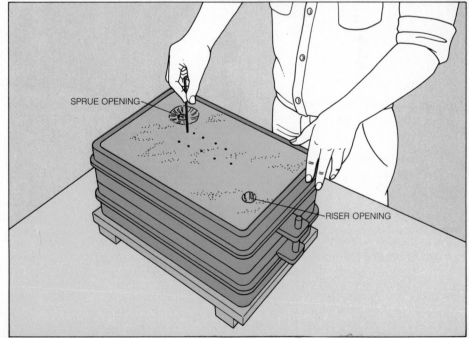

SPRUE OPENING

RISER OPENING

9 **Removing the pattern.** Before lifting the pattern from the drag, firm the pattern edge of a water-based sand mold by moistening it with a molder's bulb or a small brush dipped in water. This will help to keep the sand from collapsing when the pattern is removed. Screw draw pins into the holes in the back of the pattern and lightly tap the pattern to loosen it from the sand. Then gently pull on the draw pins, lifting the pattern straight up and out of the casting cavity.

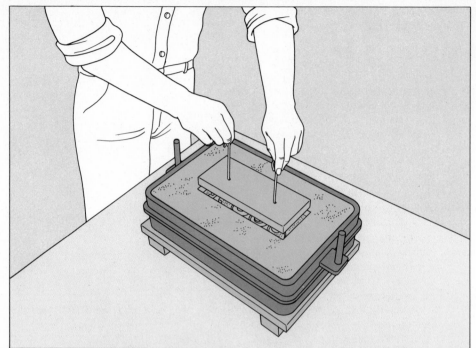

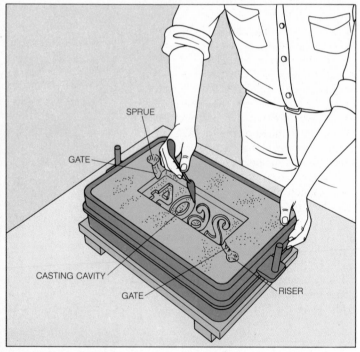

SPRUE

GATE

CASTING CAVITY

GATE

RISER

10 **Cutting the gates.** Using a piece of sheet metal bent into a ½-inch-wide U shape, cut a channel, or gate, running from the casting cavity to the riser position. Lift out a bit of sand at a time, forming a gate slightly smaller than the diameter of the riser and slightly shallower than the depth of the casting cavity. Scoop out a similar gate from the casting cavity to the sprue position. For large molds, cut several gates to the sprue and the riser from various parts of the casting cavity. Blow out or tamp down any loose bits of sand in the gates.

11 **Refining the mold.** Rebuild crumbled sections of the casting cavity by adding bits of moist sand, smoothing it into place with molding tools. Tamp down or blow away all loose sand, to prevent it from mixing with the molten metal when the metal is poured.

Replace the cope over the drag and set the flask, still on the bottom board, in the sandbox near the furnace. If you are not going to pour the casting immediately, cover the mold to keep dirt from falling into the sprue and riser.

Melting and Pouring Metal

The melting temperatures of metals vary widely. Though pewter and tin can be melted over a hotplate, the metals most often used for casting require special melting equipment. A tabletop electric furnace can be operated anywhere, but a crucible furnace like the one below, right, must be housed away from the family living quarters; it also requires its own gas and electrical attachments, as well as heavy-duty ventilation equipment to clear away heat and fumes.

Since it is not practical for most amateur metalworkers to invest in such costly equipment, metal-melting facilities are often available for use by the public at vocational-technical schools or community arts-and-crafts centers.

The melting temperatures of metals are not the same as their pouring temperatures. The pouring temperature, referred to as superheat, must be high enough above the melting temperature to ensure that the metal will not begin to solidify, or freeze off, before it has filled the mold. The degree of superheat needed varies with the type of metal and with the size and shape of the mold: Complex shapes require higher temperatures than simple ones. But be careful—if the metal is heated excessively, a coarse-grained casting may result.

When the metal heats, impurities rise to the surface as slag, which is skimmed off. Each metal has its special flux, a chemical powder that is added to it to assist in this clarifying process. Flux also breaks up gases in molten metal that can cause the mold to explode or can leave pinholes in the finished casting.

Safety in Sand Casting

When working with a helper, decide in advance who will handle each task, and follow the entire routine without interruption. Be sure to wear leather gloves and aprons, heavy leather shoes and full-face shields.

Set the mold in a box of sand (right) to catch the molten metal should the mold or crucible break.

Metal	Temperature
Pewter	420° F.
Tin	449° F.
Lead	621° F.
Zinc	787° F.
Aluminum	1,218° F.
Bronze	1,675° F.
Brass	1,700° F.
Silver	1,721° F.
Gold	1,945° F.
Copper	1,981° F.
Cast iron	2,200° F.
Steel	2,500° F.
Nickel	2,646° F.
Wrought iron	2,700° F.

Melting Temperatures

Metals and their melting points. The chart at left gives the melting points, in degrees Fahrenheit, for 14 of the metals and alloys most commonly used for casting. For molten metal to pour properly, it must be placed in a furnace that is capable of reaching temperatures higher than the metal's actual melting point.

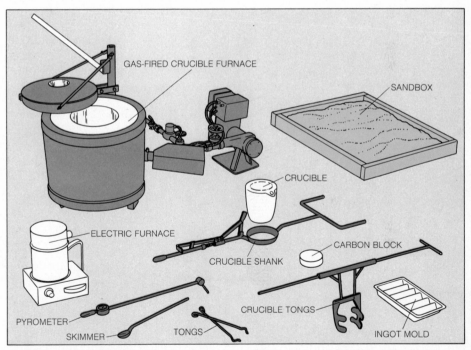

Equipment for melting metal. A typical gas fired crucible furnace (above, upper left) consists of a steel shell lined with a layer of ceramic refractory material; its flame is electronically ignited and will reach temperatures in the range of 1,200 to 2,800° F. A smaller tabletop electric furnace (above, lower left), no larger than a coffeepot, heats up to 2,000°.

Both furnaces accept a crucible—a pitcher of graphite and clay in which the metal is melted; some crucibles pour from the top, others from the bottom. Tongs are used to add metal to the crucible, and as the metal melts, its temperature is monitored with a pyrometer.

When the metal is molten, the crucible is lifted from the furnace with crucible tongs and tilted for pouring with a crucible shank; there are models for use by either one person or two. The pouring operation is done over a large, shallow sandbox, to catch spills. A carbon block, placed in the sandbox, supports the hot crucible, and the sandbox also contains, in addition to the casting mold, an ingot mold, into which the excess metal is poured after the casting mold is filled.

Pouring In the Casting

1 **Using a gas-fired crucible furnace.** Before lighting the furnace, you must load it with the charge—the metal to be melted. Place a crucible in the furnace and fill it—but do not pack it—with metal. If the crucible is packed too tightly, the charge may expand enough when heated that it will crack the crucible. Leave the furnace lid open. To light the furnace, first turn on the blower, then open the gas valve partway and adjust the air valve until the flame catches. Close the furnace lid, and after five minutes, increase both gas and air flow until the flame reaches its maximum heat; you will quickly learn to tell when this point has been reached by listening to the roar of the furnace. Check the color of the flame through the flue opening in the lid; if it is yellow, increase the air flow.

When the original charge in the crucible has melted, use tongs to add more metal as needed. Periodically insert the probe of a pyrometer through the flue opening and into the molten metal, to determine whether the metal has reached pouring temperature.

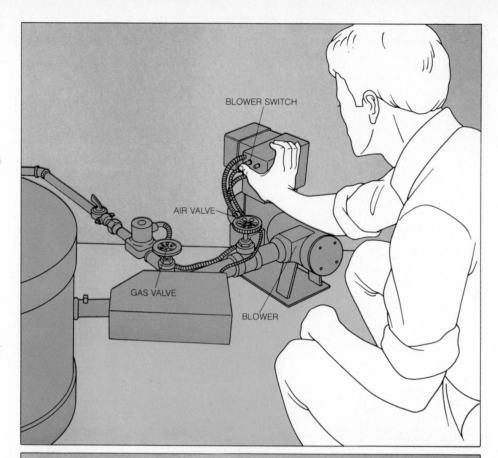

BLOWER SWITCH

AIR VALVE

GAS VALVE

BLOWER

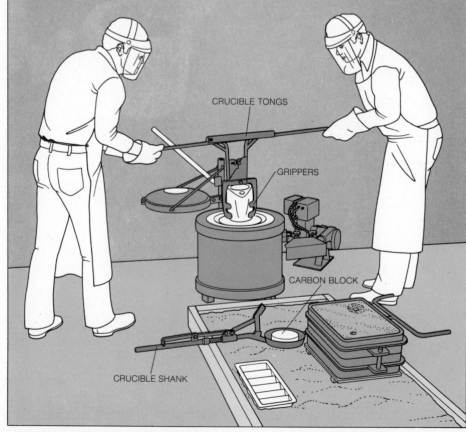

CRUCIBLE TONGS

GRIPPERS

CARBON BLOCK

CRUCIBLE SHANK

2 **Removing the crucible.** When the charge has reached the desired temperature, turn off the furnace. Before removing the crucible from the furnace, lay the crucible shank across the carbon block in the sandbox, so that it will be in place for pouring. Then slip the crucible tongs over the crucible, lock its grippers in place and, in one smooth motion, transfer the crucible from the furnace to the carbon block. Unlock the crucible tongs; store them away from the pouring area.

3 **Skimming the slag.** Using a skimmer, ladle off the impurities and oxidants, called slag, which have risen to the top of the molten metal. Dump the slag on the sand in the sandbox. Plunge a flux pellet to the bottom of the molten metal, pushing it down with the skimmer, and lightly stir the metal. Slag will again rise; skim and dump it as you did before.

If you are using a bottom-pouring crucible, there may be no need to skim the slag a second time. It is also possible to leave the slag in place when you are pouring from the top; it will act as a protective coating. But in that case your helper should hold back the slag with a metal rod called a slagging bar as you pour the metal.

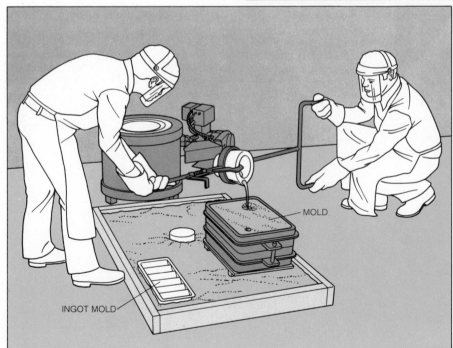

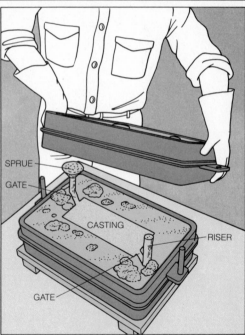

4 **Pouring the metal.** With a helper, lift the crucible shank and hook its safety lock over the lip of the crucible by pushing the latch forward. Lift and tilt the crucible a few inches above the mold, pouring the molten metal quickly and steadily into the sprue. Stop pouring when the metal nearly reaches the top of the riser. Immediately, while it is still molten, pour all the extra metal into the ingot mold. Leave the casting mold in place until the metal in the sprue and in the riser is hard; to test it, tap it with the tongs.

5 **Removing the casting.** When the metal has hardened, carry the mold to the sand-storage area. Wearing gloves, separate the cope and the drag. Lift out the hot metal casting with tongs. Break apart the sand in the mold, and dump it back into the sand-storage container. Set the casting aside to cool, leaving in place the extrusions formed by the sprue, riser and gates.

When the casting is completely cool, cut off the gates with a hacksaw; then file down the rough areas. Finish the surface as desired *(page 120).*

Surface Finishes and Repairs

The glint and gleam of metal result from the special way in which its atoms are bonded together, forming a network of crystals so small that they can be discerned only through the most powerful of microscopes. The light is mirrored by these minuscule crystals, and it plays in dazzling fashion across the tiny surface scratches created by a fine abrasive polish or the relatively coarse grooves left by the bristles of a wire brush.

But the crystalline surface can be quickly ravaged by the environment if it is not protected. The metal is vulnerable because it is no longer in its natural state—an ore that usually includes oxygen or sulfur. Having been deprived of these elements during processing, most metals quickly mix with them again when exposed to air, forming a dull and sometimes scaly skin by a corrosive electrochemical reaction called oxidation.

In some cases this layer is protective, blocking further reaction with elements in the atmosphere. Aluminum oxide, for example, bonds on the surface of an aluminum gutter in such a way that it keeps the underlying metal from oxidizing. For most metal objects, however, an oxide skin can spell disaster—fracturing, flaking or peeling off and allowing the underlying metal to oxidize further. The most common corrosion is ferric hydroxide, the rust that forms on bare iron or steel, spreading like a rash and flaking off to expose new metal to corrosion. Whenever a metal is heated, the process of oxidation accelerates: An empty copper pot allowed to remain on a hot stove develops a greenish tinge; a brass doorknob, if it is without a protective coat of lacquer or wax, turns dull brown after a few days in the blazing sun.

In the presence of water, metal is subject to another sort of corrosion: galvanic action. Just as in a car battery, the water acts as an electrolyte—a substance that conducts electricity—between the metal and its oxidized surface. Electrons are conducted between the two, converting the underlying metal to an oxide and quickening the destruction.

But as damaging as galvanic action can be, it may also serve to protect metal. Galvanized steel—a corrosion-resistant metal no modern homebuilder would be without—is produced when steel is dipped in a bath of molten zinc. Because zinc is much more susceptible to galvanic action than steel, it substitutes for the steel in a process called sacrificial corrosion. Even when the steel is opened up to corrosive elements by a nick or scratch in the zinc finish, it remains sound. The zinc contained in most rust-proofing primers and paints works, albeit less permanently, to confer the protection in the same sacrificial manner.

The Many Chores a Bench Grinder Can Handle

A bench grinder gets little rest in a metal-working shop. It sharpens cutting tools that lose their edge—cold chisels, for instance—and reshapes a chisel's relatively soft striking head, which mushrooms from repeated hammer blows. The bench grinder is also invaluable for removing rough spots from metal and for beveling and contouring metal edges in preparation for welding (page 18). Fitted with a polishing wheel, it puts a bright finish on the completed project (page 120).

A standard bench grinder has two wheels, mounted one on each side of an electric motor, plus attached tool rests and eye shields. The wheels are made of abrasive particles, usually chips of aluminum oxide, in a bonding agent. Each grain acts as a tiny cutting edge to remove metal particles from the piece being sharpened or shaped. Coarse-grained wheels (36- to 46-grit rating) are for rough cutting; fine-grained wheels (60- to 100-grit rating) are for sharpening.

Unfortunately, because of its high speed, the bench grinder can also damage tools. The friction of grinding creates so much heat that it can destroy the temper of a cutting edge. A tool being rejuvenated on a grinder should never be allowed to heat to the point where it turns blue. To guard against this, most bench grinders have a waterpot in which tools can be dipped, or quenched, for cooling; it should be kept filled.

After much use, the face of a grinding wheel can lose efficiency in any of three ways. The grains can become dulled, giving the wheel a glazed look. The spaces between grains can fill with metal shards; in this condition the wheel is referred to as loaded. Or the wheel face can develop high spots and furrows.

When any of these conditions occur, the wheel must be resurfaced—the spoiled surface scraped away and the unused grains beneath exposed. This process can be repeated as often as needed, until the diameter of the wheel is reduced by an inch. Two companion procedures for improving the wheel face—shearing, or dressing, and leveling, or truing—are done with any of several instruments; the most common is the star wheel-dresser, a device with star-shaped hardened-steel disks at one end.

Occasionally a grinding wheel will chip or crack. It must be replaced immediately. A cracked or chipped wheel, or even one that has been dropped and shows no visible damage, can explode into fragments when run at full speed. To guard against such a dangerous occurrence, and to avoid the sparks and grit that accompany metal grinding, always lower the eye shield on the grinder and protect your eyes with safety goggles. In addition, do not operate a grinder without a wheel guard, and always position yourself at one side of the wheel rather than directly in front of it.

As further precautions in controlling the work, position the tool rest no more than ⅛ inch away from the wheel face, and keep your hands free of oil.

A Quick Shape-up for a Dull Cold Chisel

1 **Setting the tool rest.** Loosen the wing nut that holds the tool rest, and place the chisel shaft flat against the rest. Adjust the angle of the rest until one bevel of the chisel's cutting edge is flush with the face of the grinding wheel, at a point on the upper half of the wheel. Check to make sure that the front edge of the tool rest is no more than ⅛ inch from the wheel face; then tighten the wing nut and remove the chisel.

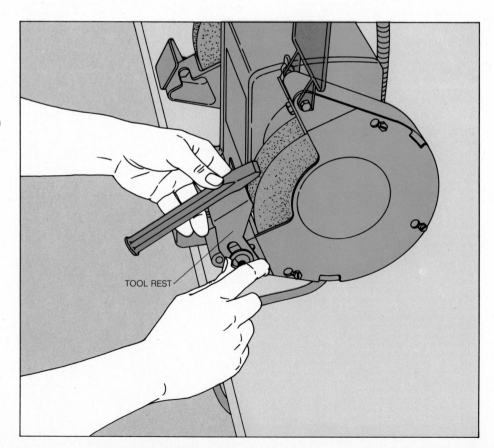

TOOL REST

2 **Grinding the cutting surfaces.** Turn on the grinder, and when the wheel has reached full speed, place the chisel on the tool rest. Bring one of the beveled surfaces into light contact with the wheel face and move the chisel slowly left and right. Grind one beveled surface, then the other, quenching the cutting edge frequently by dipping it into the grinder's waterpot. Examine the beveled surfaces for a smooth, uniform finish. Then check the angle of the cutting edge with a protractor; the two beveled faces together should create an angle of 60° *(inset)*.

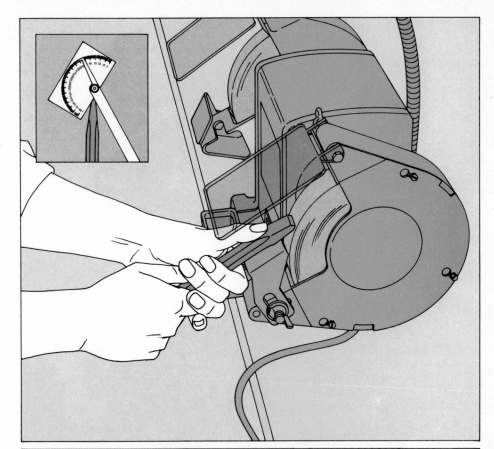

3 **Restoring the shape of the striking head.** With the grinder running, hold the chisel at a 45° angle to the wheel face and bring the splayed end of the striking head in contact with the wheel. Slowly rotate the tool clockwise to remove the deformed metal, tapering the head inward about 15° *(inset)*. Quench frequently to keep the metal from becoming hot. Quenching it when it is hot will temper the end, making it brittle and thus likely to chip when it is struck with a hammer.

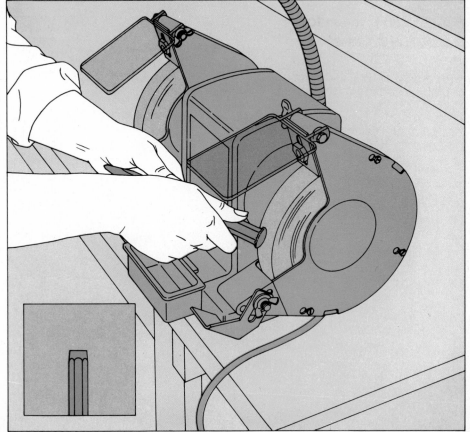

Restoring a Punch Point

Grinding the angle. With the grinder on, bring the cone-shaped point in contact with the wheel. Slowly rotate the punch clockwise a full 360°. Then use a protractor to check the angle of the cone; for a center punch it should be 90°, for a prick punch 30°. Continue grinding until the angle is correct, quenching the tool frequently so that it will not get overheated.

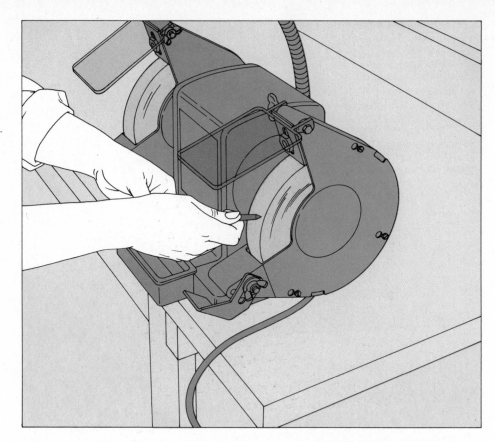

A Worn Grinding Wheel Dressed and Made True

1 **Adjusting the tool rest.** Loosen the tool-rest wing nut, and slide the tool rest away from the wheel until the head of a star wheel-dresser will fit in between the tool rest and the wheel. With the motor turned off, make sure the bottom lip of the dresser head is hooked over the edge of the tool rest; then tighten the wing nut.

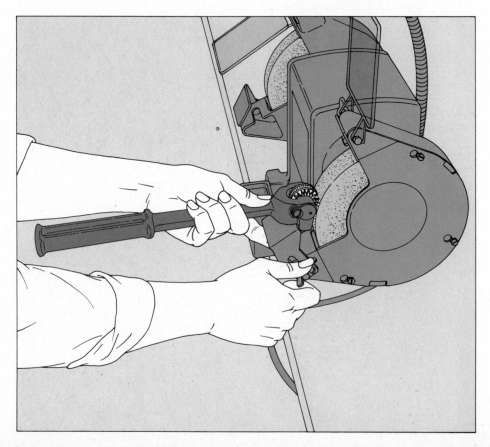

2 **Dressing and truing the wheel.** With the grinding wheel on, grasp the dresser handle firmly with both hands and slowly raise the handle, lowering the cutting head until the cutters make full contact with the wheel face. Apply firm, even pressure and move the cutting head slowly from side to side, adjusting pressure on the tool so that it produces a minimum of sparks. Continue cutting the wheel until a new layer of grit has been exposed, stopping the wheel occasionally to check your progress. When properly dressed and trued, the wheel face should be of uniform color, without metallic or shiny patches. Run your fingers across the stopped wheel face; it should have no grooves or high spots.

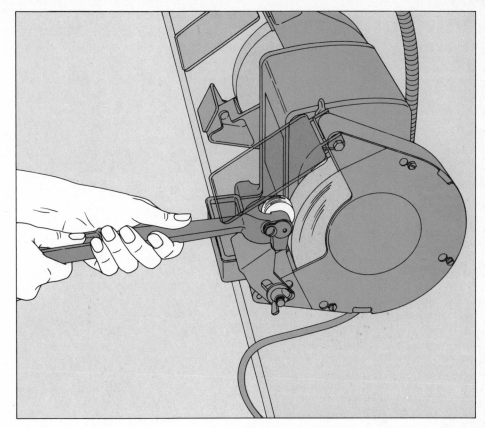

Mounting a New Wheel

Procedures for changing a wheel. A grinding wheel is fastened to its shaft by two metal flanges that fit against cardboard disks, often called the blotters, pressed to both sides of the wheel. The assembly is held by a machine nut. The nut on the right wheel loosens counterclockwise; the one on the left clockwise. A wheel guard, screwed to the body of the grinder, protects the outer face of the wheel.

Before mounting a new wheel, examine it for cracks and chips. To test it for hidden flaws, suspend the wheel on a dowel or a pencil and tap the wheel face lightly with a screwdriver handle; you should hear a solid, bell-like tone. If the wheel is sound, mount it as above, tightening the nuts just enough to keep it from slipping.

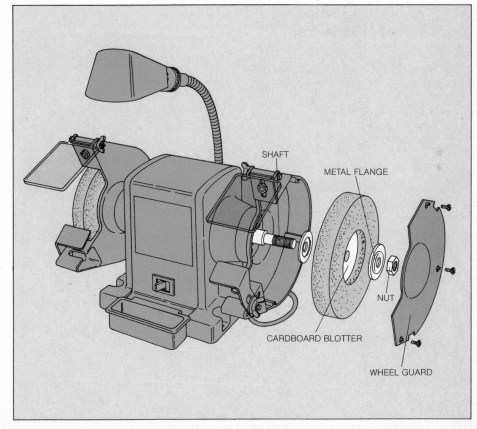

SHAFT

METAL FLANGE

NUT

CARDBOARD BLOTTER

WHEEL GUARD

Polishing, Buffing and Texturing Surfaces

As a final step in its fabrication, metal is usually polished to remove deposits, gouges and imperfections left by welding, soldering and cutting. By the gradual progression from coarse abrasives to finer ones, a smooth surface is attained, which can then be finished in a variety of ways. If the metal is to be painted, it is generally rough-finished, providing a grainy surface to which paint will adhere. If the metal is to be left exposed, it can be polished to a high luster and buffed to a final sheen, or it can be textured with specialized finishing techniques—brushing, graining, peening and spot polishing. Brushing and graining produce a finely lined satin finish and are often associated with specific metals. Aluminum and brass are commonly brushed, for example, and graining is a useful technique for restoring the finish on worn stainless steel. Peening, done with a hammer, pocks the surface of the metal with light-reflecting dimples, and spot polishing makes use of a hand-held drill or a drill press fitted with a wooden dowel to cover the metal surface with light-reflecting circles.

The gradual process of reducing a metal surface from rough to smooth can often be done by hand by means of sandpaper, emery cloth, abrasive powders or steel wool. But power tools speed the work. The fastest polishing tool is probably the sandblaster, which is especially useful for rough-finishing large areas that are going to be painted later. Used with heavy sand grit, the sandblaster can make quick work of removing rust, aluminum oxides and old paint, for example. But when its canister is filled instead with light sand grit or tiny glass beads, it will produce a very fine polished finish. Equipment for sandblasting is usually available at tool-rental stores and is normally powered by an air compressor that runs on ordinary household current.

Other power tools that do an efficient job of polishing include the standard hand-held electric drill and the bench grinder. The drill can be fitted with such metal-polishing attachments as sanding disks, wire brushes and buffing wheels; and the hard abrasive wheels of the grinder can be replaced with wheels of cloth, leather or felt. For purists, there are also special power buffers, both hand-held and stationary.

Because polishing and buffing wheels are soft, they tend to splay when a hard object is held against them as they spin. If you use a bench grinder fitted with such wheels, you can remove the cast-iron plate that covers the outer face of the wheel as shown on page 121, bottom left, to give the wheel some extra room. If you are polishing large objects that require the wheel to be fully exposed, you can remove the entire cast-iron guard that covers the top, bottom and back of the wheel: Unscrew the bolts that fasten the guard to the body of the machine. If you do remove the entire guard, set up a cardboard or sheet-metal backsplash to protect nearby walls.

Before being used, soft buffing wheels are coated with polishing compounds. The four most commonly used are natural materials—pumice, tripoli, rouge and whiting. Pumice, made from powdered lava, and tripoli, from decomposed limestone, are both used for preliminary polishing. Rouge, made from red iron oxide, and whiting, from pulverized chalk, are used for buffing to a high sheen.

These compounds, and many other commercial variations, are sold in block or bar form and are applied by being held against the spinning wheel. They should be applied sparingly, to avoid a heavy build-up on the wheel and ultimately on the metal. Should the latter occur, you can remove excess polishing compound by cleaning the metal with alcohol or a solution of hot water and washing soda.

A separate wheel should be used for each polishing compound. If you put different compounds on the same wheel, you will cancel out their special abrasive effects. For the same reason, the metal should be cleaned, as described above, whenever you switch from one polishing compound to another.

Prior to being polished, metal surfaces should be stripped of protective lacquer coatings, which are often put on by manufacturers to prevent metals such as brass and copper from oxidizing on exposure to air. These can be removed with lacquer thinner, which should be rubbed on with a soft clean cloth.

For safety, always hold a metal object against the lower front of the spinning wheel. If you hold it against the top of the wheel, the object could be wrested from your hands and could fly up and hit you. When polishing with an electric drill, be sure the metal object is held securely. It is safe to hold small objects such as door knobs in your hand, and very large objects are often stabilized by their own weight, provided they are resting on a sturdy work surface. But other objects should be anchored in a vise or held by wood blocks clamped or nailed to a worktable.

As in all metalwork, it is vitally important in polishing to protect your body from flying metal particles. Always wear full-coverage safety goggles and a pair of sturdy gloves. In sandblasting, always follow the manufacturer's instructions to the letter. Sandblasting requires a respirator as well as the customary coverage for eyes and other exposed parts of the body. And never put your hands in front of the nozzle of the sandblaster while it is in operation—the abrasive spray leaves the nozzle at a extremely high velocity.

Rough Polishing
with a Sandblaster

Creating a rough-polished surface. Place a
dropcloth at the base of the metal to be sandblast-
ed, and grasp the underside of the sandblaster
canister firmly with one hand while holding the
handle-and-trigger assembly with the other.
With the blast nozzle held 1 to 2 feet away from
the surface, aim the nozzle and pull the trigger
to blow the abrasive directly against the metal.
Move the canister up and down sideways,
until one area of the surface is clear, refilling the
canister with fresh abrasive as needed.

For a smoother finish, refill the canister with
the used abrasive that has collected on the dropcloth, and blast the same area again. As the
abrasive gets finer with repeated use, the surface
texture of the metal will become smoother.

Fine Polishing with a Buffing Wheel

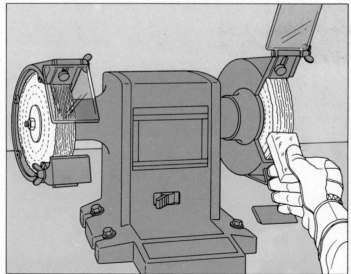

1 **Preparing the wheel for polishing.** Wearing
gloves to protect your hands from heat produced
by friction, hold the bar of polishing compound
against the lower front portion of the buffing wheel as it spins. Coat the wheel lightly and
evenly with the compound.

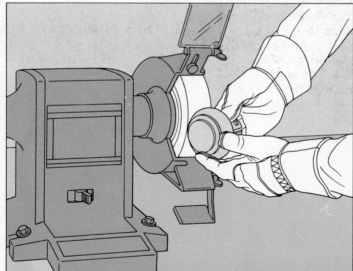

2 **Buffing the metal.** Grasp the object to be buffed
firmly in both hands, and hold it lightly against
the lower front of the polish-coated buffing wheel.
Move the object constantly back and forth,
and turn it to ensure a smooth, even finish over
the entire surface. When the finish is uniform
in appearance, clean the metal *(page 120)* and, if
desired, change to a wheel coated with a finer
polishing compound. Repeat the polishing procedure, again cleaning the metal after polishing.
If a still higher gloss is desired, change wheels to
one coated with a still finer abrasive, then
clean the metal again and finally buff it with a
leather wheel used without any abrasive.

Polishing the Old to Look Like New

Graining stainless steel. To grain worn stainless steel, use silicon-carbide wet-or-dry paper with at least a No. 100 grit. Insert the paper into a rubber sandpaper holder and, after wetting the metal surface, push the abrasive paper over the metal in long, straight, even strokes, using steady pressure *(below, left).* Keep the metal surface wet at all times. In corners and along curves, use your hand rather than the rubber block to shape and guide the abrasive paper *(below, right).* For the best finish, be consistent in the direction and length of the strokes.

Creative Methods to Decorate Surfaces

Spot polishing. Fit a 2- to 3-inch length of wooden dowel into the chuck of a drill press or a hand-held electric drill. Choose a dowel whose diameter will produce the desired mark, and sand the dowel end smooth and flat. Dip the end of the dowel in valve-grinding compound, a gritty paste available at automotive-supply stores. Anchor the metal object with one hand or a clamp while you gently lower the spinning dowel briefly against the surface. Raise the dowel after each impression, and move the metal object slightly to create a jewel-like pattern of overlapping circles *(inset),* adding more compound to the dowel when necessary.

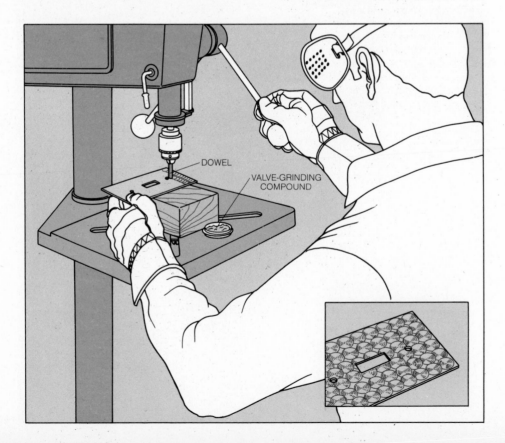

DOWEL

VALVE-GRINDING COMPOUND

Brushed texturing. Secure the metal object between the jaws of a vise. For objects too large for a vise, use protective wooden blocks clamped to the work surface. Fit a wire-brush attachment onto a hand-held electric drill and, holding the drill firmly with both hands, move the spinning brush back and forth over the metal surface in smooth parallel strokes. Wipe the metal occasionally with a piece of cloth to observe the progress being made. Softer metals, such as aluminum, brass and copper, will need less pressure than steel for a smooth brushed surface, and should therefore be checked more often.

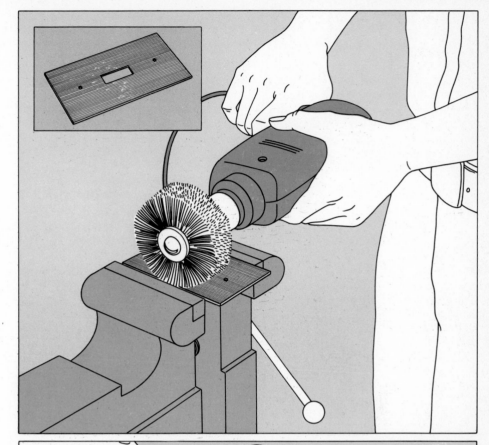

Peening a metal surface. Using a ball-peen hammer and a metal surface as an anvil, strike the metal object repeatedly with the rounded end of the hammer. Keep the strokes regular so that the indentations are fairly even in depth, and place the strokes close together so that the entire surface is textured. For hard-to-reach places, use a solid punch, struck with a ball-peen hammer, to make the indentations.

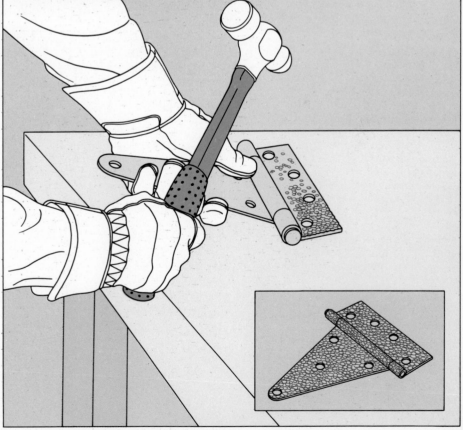

Using Heat or Chemicals to Change Metal Color

In contrast to the alchemists who vainly sought to turn base metal into gold *(page 127)*, modern metalworkers perform all sorts of real transformational magic. Using heat, chemicals and electricity, they can change the colors of many metals or make one metal look like another. Practical applications for this art are concerned primarily with decorating and refurbishing small objects such as switch plates and doorknobs, or with antiquing copper roof flashing or window boxes.

Any metal containing iron—notably steel—can be colored with the oven heat of an ordinary kitchen range. Depending on the temperature setting, the steel will change color across a spectrum of shades ranging from pale yellow to dark blue *(below)*. In addition, literally hundreds of chemicals will change the color of metal surfaces. Some of them are too toxic for amateurs to use—for example, cyanides, nitric acid, chromic acid, mercuric chloride and lead acetate. There are others, available from hobby shops, pharmacies and chemical distributors, that can be used safely.

There are two ways to color with chemicals. For the most even coating, objects should be dipped into a chemical bath. However, when objects are too large to be dipped or are not movable, they can be coated with a brush.

Mix the chemicals in a glass or porcelain container. For safety, always wear rubber gloves, a rubber apron and goggles, and work either outdoors or in a room ventilated with a fan. When you are ready to dispose of the chemicals, used or unused, consult local or state pollution-control authorities.

Metals colored by electroplating *(page 126)* have the most durable coating. In this process, applicable to all metals, a plating solution containing positively charged metal particles is brushed across a negatively charged metal surface, which bonds the particles to itself. A 12-volt car battery can be used to charge both the metal surface and the plating solution, and a carbon core taken from a flashlight battery will serve as a brush. Plating solutions come in an array of metals, the most common of which are brass, nickel, silver and chrome—and in alloys that produce gradations of color.

Whatever the coloring method, the metal surface must first be cleaned of any oxidation. Begin by washing the surface with water and a dishwashing detergent, then rinse it thoroughly and dip the metal briefly into a pickling solution of 1 part sulphuric acid to 10 parts water. Then rinse it in water. For safety during this operation, wear rubber gloves, goggles and a rubber apron, and always pour the sulphuric acid slowly into the water, never the reverse.

Less hazardous than cleaning with acid, but also less effective, are two alternatives. You can grind away the oxidation with pumice *(page 121)*, or you can brush on soldering flux *(page 60)* to dissolve the oxidation. After using flux, wash away the residue with soap and water. No matter what method you use to clean the surface of the metal, though, you will have to test it afterward. When the metal is clean enough for coloring, water sprinkled on it will not bead up on the surface.

Adjusting the Oven to Make Colored Steel

Choosing the right temperature. Set the oven temperature for the color you want, using the gradations in the column at the right as a guide. Monitor the oven temperature with an oven thermometer, making sure the correct temperature has been reached before you insert the object. Check the object periodically; when the metal's temperature reaches that of the oven, the metal will turn the color desired.

The coloring can be stopped and then resumed, but never reversed. If the steel goes beyond the color desired, you will have to remove the surface of the metal with an abrasive polish *(page 121)* and start all over again.

Color	Temperature
Very pale yellow	430° F.
Light yellow	440° F.
Pale straw yellow	450° F.
Straw yellow	460° F.
Deep straw yellow	470° F.
Dark yellow	480° F.
Yellow brown	490° F.
Brown	500° F.
Spotted reddish brown	510° F.
Purple brown	520° F.
Light purple	530° F.
Purple	540° F.
Dark purple	550° F.
Blue	560° F.
Dark blue	570° F.

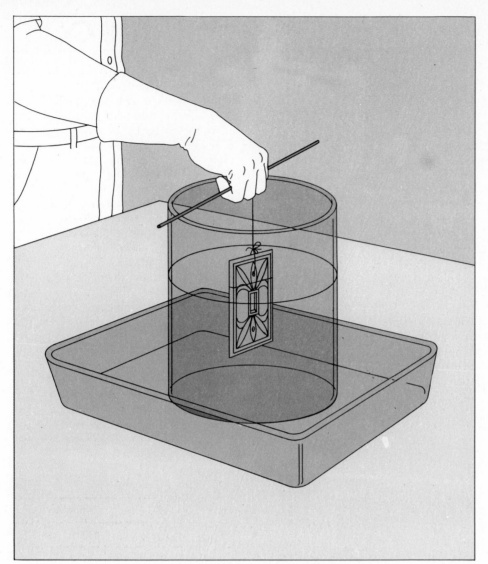

A Method of Suspending an Object in Solution

Dipping metals safely. Set a glass beaker inside a plastic pan large enough to hold the coloring solution if the beaker should break. Attach one end of a nylon line to the metal object, the other end to a section of wire coat hanger long enough to span the top of the container. The nylon line should be short enough to hold the object suspended within the coloring solution. Lower the object into the solution, and leave it there until it has reached the desired shade. Then lift it out, and rinse it as indicated in the recipe *(below)*. To protect the finish when it is dry, either brush or spray on clear lacquer.

To highlight raised detail, rub these areas of the newly colored surface with fine steel wool before applying the lacquer.

Recipes for Coloring Copper, Steel or Aluminum

Copper, Brass and Bronze

☐ RED. Mix 1 teaspoon of copper carbonate, 10 teaspoons of household ammonia and 1 teaspoon of sodium carbonate into a quart of boiling water. Dip the object to be colored briefly into this solution, just until the metal turns bright red. Rinse the metal first in cold water, then in a pickling solution of sulfuric acid *(text, opposite)*, then again in cold water.

☐ ANTIQUE GREEN. Mix 3 parts of copper carbonate to 1 part sal ammoniac (a type of soldering flux), 1 part copper acetate, 1 part cream of tartar and 8 parts acetic acid. Brush the solution on the metal; it will take several days for the weathered-green patina to appear.

☐ BROWN. Mix 2 teaspoons of potassium sulfate, 3 teaspoons of lye and 1 quart of hot water. Dip the object into this solution, and leave it there until the desired shade is achieved, then rinse the metal in cold water.

☐ BLACK. Mix 1 tablespoon of liver of sulfur and a rounded ¼ teaspoon of ammonia in 1 quart of cold water. Immerse the object in the solution until the desired shade is achieved, then rinse the metal in cold water.

Iron and Steel

☐ BLACK. Mix ¾ cup of tannic acid into 1 quart of cold water. Dip the object in the solution until it turns black, then rinse in cold water.

Aluminum Alloys

☐ ALL COLORS. Dip the object into a solution of 2 tablespoons of lye to 1 quart of cold water for one to two minutes. Then immerse the metal in household dye of the desired color, mixed according to the manufacturer's instructions. When the desired depth of color is achieved, rinse in cold water.

Coating Metal with Metal by Electroplating

1 **Setting up an electroplating device.** Using a battery cable, connect the metal object to be plated to the negative terminal of a 12-volt car battery. Then make an electroplating brush by extracting the carbon core from a Size D battery—the type used in flashlights. To break open the battery, hit it with a hammer. Wipe off the core, and clip a battery cable to one end of it. Wrap sterilized cotton around the other end of the core *(inset)*, and secure the cotton with electrical tape. Then tape the rest of the core and the clip, to provide a protective handle for the brush. Finally, clip the other end of the brush cable to the positive terminal of the car battery.

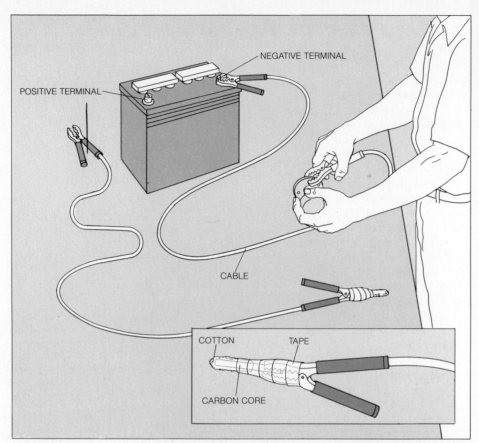

2 **Plating the metal.** Wearing rubber gloves, dip the electroplating brush into the plating solution for five seconds, until the cotton-wrapped tip is saturated. Touch the tip to the surface of the metal object and, with a circular motion, spread the solution over a small area for about 25 seconds. Repeat this procedure until you have plated the entire surface.

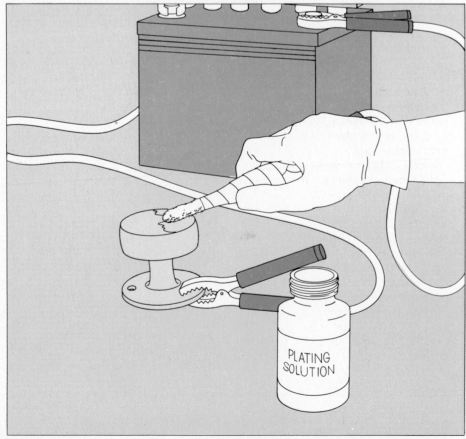

A Search for Gold: The Ancient Art of Alchemy

Although the apparent transformation of steel into gold by electroplating *(opposite)* may seem remarkable to people today, it probably would not have startled our ancestors: They were constantly being promised a breakthrough in the art of alchemy—a mystical effort to create gold from base metals. From the First Century A.D. to the 17th, scholars all over the world labored in the service of this dream. The alchemists never succeeded, of course, but they helped develop many of the techniques of modern metallurgy.

Alchemy grew out of Greek, Arabic and Chinese philosophies. Some mystics believed that metals were alive and went through a process of natural purification on the way to becoming gold, the perfect substance. Subscribers to this school of alchemy thought that if only they could imitate nature well enough in their laboratories—in part by prolonged grinding up of ores with a mortar and pestle to simulate erosion—they could hasten this evolution. Others believed all metals contained the same essence, a seed that could grow into gold, and that if they killed a metal with fire, it might be reborn as gold.

Chinese alchemists advanced the idea that adding a particular substance to a base metal would bring about the desired change; finding this substance, called the philosophers' stone, became an alchemists' goal.

Several alchemists promoted the theory that transmutation of a base metal into gold required twelve steps—among them, distillation to separate the subject material into its component parts and thus release its "primary essence." Even astrology had a role; the alchemists would sometimes schedule certain steps to coincide with what they saw as appropriate celestial influences.

Most alchemists were sincerely motivated—seeking after nature's truths, or seeking to alleviate poverty. Some, however, were get-rich-quick artists who swindled wealthy believers by faking transmutations. Typically, a charlatan gulled his victim by boiling a crucible of mercury in a furnace and then mixing in some chalk or lead powder that claimed to be the philosophers' stone. To this concoction he added a lump of coal, secretly filled with gold powder held in with wax. As the wax melted, the gold ran out of the coal; at the same time, the mercury evaporated, leaving gold in its place in the crucible. The astonished onlooker eagerly paid a huge sum to get the recipe, whereupon the fake alchemist quickly left town.

Testimonies from reputable people claiming to have witnessed a transmutation kept the pseudo-science alive—although the alchemists themselves had a dismally low survival rate. Some lost their heads for refusing to divulge their trade secrets, some succumbed to their own toxic fumes, and a few unlucky charlatans were lynched.

Around the year 1600, alchemy began to die out, as modern science with its systematic methods of observation became established. But by that time the alchemists had bequeathed a priceless legacy: not gold, but methods of gilding, casting and alloying that are still used by metallurgists.

An alchemist at work. In this 17th Century woodcut, an alchemist mixes ingredients that he hopes will turn to gold. Other substances bubble in his laboratory furnace, called an athanor.

Preventing and Repairing Corrosion Damage

For all their toughness, metals are constantly subject to surface damage: Dents, holes, rust and tarnish can blemish almost any metal. But with careful protection or simple repairs, you can retain or restore the original luster.

The most common ravager of metal is the atmosphere. Oxygen and such airborne chemicals as salts and acids react with a metal's surface to turn its smoothness flaky. The most widespread form of corrosion is rust, the result of moist air interacting with iron and steel to form hydrated ferric oxide. Galvanized metals also rust, but at a slower rate unless the galvanized coating is damaged. Brass, silver and bronze tarnish as they interact with the atmosphere. Aluminum oxidizes into a white powder, although the powder binds chemically to the metal beneath, blocking further corrosion.

To prevent iron railings, gutters, metal roofs and the like from corroding, their surfaces must be sealed from the air by protective coatings. Mainly these are paints and their primers; but waxes, oils and lacquers are also used.

Primers are special paints made to seal out air while serving as bridges to tougher, more durable finishing paints. Some have pigments ground so fine they actually penetrate into the metal. Others have additives for special situations or certain metals. Examples are an oil-based primer containing finely ground portland cement that protects iron and steel; a zinc-rich primer that, on bare metal, imitates the factory-applied protective zinc covering of galvanized steel; and a zinc-dust primer that serves as a bridge between the zinc of galvanized steel and finishing coats to be laid on top.

Manufacturers also make combination primer-finish paints, sometimes called metal paints, that are used mainly on iron and steel. These paints combine a primer with a colored finish paint in one can, but they do not wear as well as regular paint applied over a primer.

Finish paints for metals come in the standard types—latex, oil and alkyd—but

Protecting the Surface with Primer and Paint

Metal	Oil primer	Alkyd primer	Latex primer	Oil-cement primer	Zinc-rich primer	Zinc-dust primer	Aluminum paint	Combination primer/paint	Glossy oil paint	Glossy alkyd paint	Glossy latex paint	Flat oil paint	Flat alkyd paint	Flat latex paint	Epoxy paint	Urethane paint	Epoxy varnish	Polyurethane varnish	Acrylic lacquer	Mineral or linseed oil	Acrylic or paste wax
Iron or steel	●	●	●	●	●		●	●	●	●					●		●		●	●	
Galvanized metal	○	○	○	●	●	●															
Aluminum	●	●	●		●		●		●	●	●	●	●	●	●	●	●	●	●	●	
Copper, bronze or brass		●			●											●	●	●	●		●

● Denotes compatible coating for metal specified.
○ Use a type formulated for galvanized metal.

The right coating for the job. The chart above pairs metals, listed vertically, with compatible coatings, listed across the top, progressing from primers to paints to clear finishes. When you buy oil, alkyd or latex paints, choose one formulated especially for metal and, depending on the job, one specified for interior or exterior application. When you use primers with paints, choose a pair that are compatible; if you have doubts, ask your paint dealer.

they are specially formulated to include corrosion inhibitors and should be used instead of the ones made for wood. Besides these, urethane paints and epoxy paints—both highly resistant to chemicals and weather—can be used on metal, although urethane vapors require caution. Of the epoxies, the toughest come in two containers; the resin in one and the hardener in the other are mixed just before the paint is used. A good waterproofer is a paint with powdered aluminum added—it can be used on several metals, including aluminum, which does not have to be painted but may become pitted if left untreated.

Among clear finishes, epoxy and polyurethane varnishes provide particularly durable coatings. Lacquer, often industrially applied over products such as door hardware, is less durable; but the worn coating is easily removed with lacquer thinner, and a new coating applied. Oils are good coatings for tools, and although they wear away quickly, they are quickly reapplied. Waxes, as well as lacquers and clear varnishes, can be used on copper, brass and bronze to prevent tarnishing; acrylic waxes generally wear longer and remain clearer than paste waxes.

To get the best protection from any coating, clean all rust, dirt, loose paint or tarnish from the surface of the metal to be coated. Chemical strippers are the preferred cleansing agent for silver and brass; on iron and steel, it may be faster to abrade the surface with a paint scraper, a wire brush or sandpaper until the surface is clean. To apply coatings, you can use brushes, rollers, spray cans, spray guns, or cloths; for shaped iron railings, plastic-lined mitten applicators can be dipped directly into paint without soiling the hand within.

Dents and holes also mar the surfaces of metal, but simple techniques can be used to repair the damage. Dents in thin or decorative metals can usually be hammered out to the original shape. If bumps remain, the damaged area must be reheated and the metal reshaped.

Depressions and holes in painted surfaces, usually iron and steel, can be filled with auto-body fillers, sold in kits containing applicators, fiberglass screening and epoxy ingredients. Once sanded, the filler is painted with the same type of primer and paint used on the surrounding metal. For a large hole, a soldered-on metal patch is the best remedy.

Wire Brushes to Remove Rust and Dirt

Using an electric drill. Fit a wire-brush attachment to an electric drill and, wearing goggles, abrade the metal at high speed to dislodge rust and loose paint. Continue until the surface is smooth; you need not remove paint that is still well bonded. Use cup- or spindle-shaped wire-brush attachments (inset) for cleaning inside curves and other intricate metalwork. Once the metal is smooth, you can sand it with silicon-carbide sandpaper, grits 40 (coarse) to 320 (extra fine), if you want it even smoother. Wipe the surface clean with a soft cloth dipped in rubbing alcohol, then apply the coating of your choice.

A Patch for a Small Hole

1 Preparing the hole. Clear a border at least 1 inch wide around the hole on both sides by using coarse sandpaper to remove paint, rust, oil and dirt from the surrounding metal. Leave the surface rough but clean. On the back side of the metal, use a putty knife or the applicator supplied with the kit to coat the border with epoxy filler, mixed as specified by the manufacturer. Then use a putty knife to press into the epoxy the edges of a piece of fiberglass screening, cut 1 inch larger than the hole. Let the epoxy cure, following the maker's instructions.

2 Filling the hole. Working from the front side and using the kit applicator, a putty knife or even a stiff piece of cardboard, cover the screening with epoxy. Apply epoxy until the hole is filled. Then build up the epoxy above the surface of the metal and let it slightly overlap the edges of the hole. Allow the epoxy to cure.

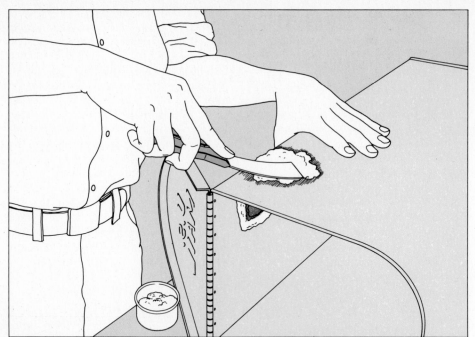

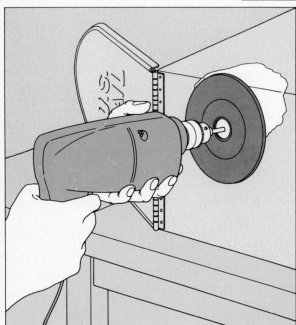

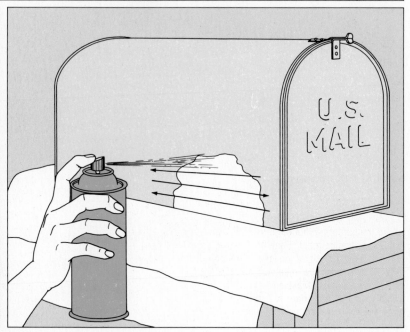

3 Sanding the patch. Use rough (about 40-grit) silicon-carbide sandpaper to reduce the built-up dry epoxy to the level of the surrounding metal; a power sander will speed the job. Then use 80-grit sandpaper followed by 200- or 300-grit to make the patch glass-smooth.

4 Coating the patch. To remove dust and grit, wipe the patch with a soft cloth soaked in rubbing alcohol. Spray the patch with primer, holding the can approximately 6 inches from the surface of the metal and moving it slowly from side to side in a straight line, not in an arc.

Sand the primer surface with 300-grit wet-and-dry silicon-carbide sandpaper dipped in water. Then wipe the surface again with an alcohol-dipped cloth, and spray on a finishing coat of paint. When the paint has dried, sand the surface again, clean it and apply a second coat of finishing paint. Then, once this coat has dried, buff the surface with a soft, clean cloth.

Patching Over a Large Hole

1 **Making a metal patch.** To repair a large hole, such as one that might develop in a galvanized-tin roof, cut a piece of sheet metal twice as large as the hole; mark a rectangle within the piece that allows 1-inch borders beyond the hole's edges. Snip the corners *(inset),* then bend the borders by placing them, one at a time, under a board and pulling the sheet metal up *(right).* Then, using a ball-peen hammer, flatten the borders toward the center of the patch *(bottom right).*

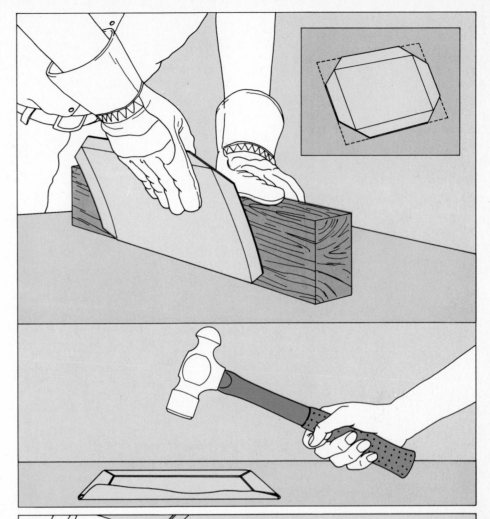

2 **Soldering with a propane torch.** Remove paint, oil, dirt and rust for 2 inches around the hole by cleaning and tinning as described on page 61. Fit the patch over the hole, and gently pound the borders with a hammer to fit them to the surrounding metal. Paint a thin layer of flux around the edges; solder the joint with a propane torch, heating the metal just ahead of the solder being applied. Make sure the solder is smooth and that it overlaps the joint completely on all sides. Then wipe the edges clean, and coat the entire area with a rust-preventive primer before painting with a finish coat.

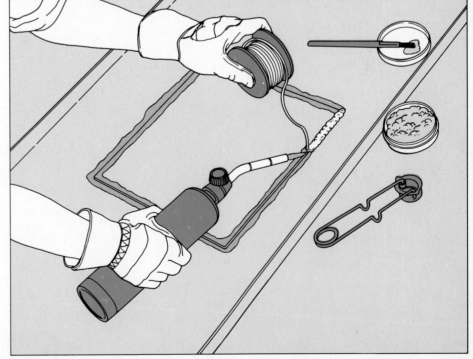

Malleting Out Small Dents

Using a sandbag. Place an easy-to-reach dented area against a plastic or cloth bag filled with sand. Then gently tap the dent with a wooden or rubber mallet until the metal has been restored to its original shape.

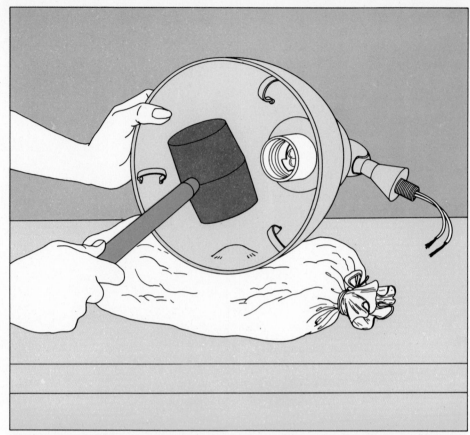

Using a stake. If you cannot hit the high side of a dent directly, clamp a wooden stake in a vise. Position the dented object over the stake so that you can press the dent against the top end of the stake. Tap the side of the stake gently with a ball-peen hamer; the vibrations of the stake will gradually pound out the dent.

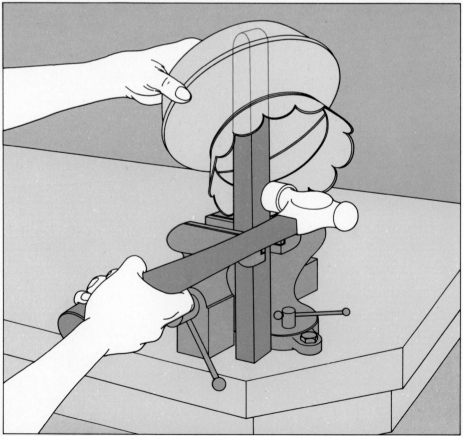

Filler for a Dent That Cannot Be Malleted

1 **Drilling anchor holes.** If you cannot reach the back of a dent with a hammer or a stake because a double layer of metal has been used, sand the dent and a 1-inch area around it, exposing the bare metal. Drill ⅛-inch holes ½-inch apart in the dent, being careful that you do not drill through the inside layer of metal.

2 **Applying the filler.** Using a putty knife or other applicator, fill the dent with an epoxy mixture, pressing the epoxy into the drilled holes so that some of it is spread onto the inaccessible side of the metal. Build the filler slightly higher than the surface of the surrounding metal, and overlap the edges of the dented area. Allow the epoxy to cure completely, then sand it to the level of the original surface. Clean and paint the filler as on page 130, Steps 3 and 4.

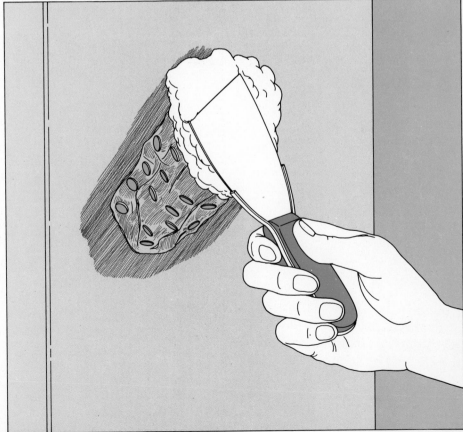

Picture Credits

The sources for the illustrations in this book are shown below. The drawings were created by Jack Arthur, Roger Essley, Chuck Forsythe, William J. Hennessy Jr., John Jones, Dick Lee, John Martinez and Joan McGurren. Credits for the illustrations from left to right are separated by semicolons, from top to bottom by dashes.

Cover: Fil Hunter. 6: Fil Hunter. 10, 11: Arezou Katoozian. 12-19: Elsie J. Hennig. 20-23: Edward L. Cooper. 24-27: Frederic F. Bigio from B-C Graphics. 28-35: Arezou Katoozian. 36: Fil Hunter. 38-42: Susan Strok. 43-47: Elsie J. Hennig. 49-55: John Massey. 56, 57: Arezou Katoozian. 58: Fil Hunter. 60-63: Walter Hilmers Jr. from H-J Commercial Art. 65-71: Eduino J. Pereira from Arts and Words. 73-85: William J. Hennessy Jr. 87, 88: Frederic F. Bigio from B-C Graphics. 89: Frederic F. Bigio from B-C Graphics—Courtesy the Lincoln Electric Company. 90-95: Frederic F. Bigio from B-C Graphics. 97: Carla de Benedetti, Milan, Rosanna Monzini, architect. 98: Lewis H. Dreyer from the Gil Amiaga Collection—Norman McGrath, Peter de Bretteville, architect. 99: Carla de Benedetti, Milan, Piero Pinto, architect—Ron Sutherland from Elizabeth Whiting and Associates, London. 100, 101: ©Cervin Robinson; Carla de Benedetti, Milan, Marc Held, architect—©Robert Perron, 1980, Circus Studios Ltd., architects; Carla de Benedetti, Milan, Helmut Schulitz, architect. 102: Charles Wiesehahn—P. Hinous, Connaissance des Arts, Paris, Carla Venosta, designer. 103: Leonard Nones, Alan Buchsbaum, architect—Norman McGrath, Marlys Hann, architect; ©Robert Perron, 1980, Circus Studios Ltd., architects. 104: Brecht-Einzig, Ltd., London, Max Clendinning, architect. 105: Jack Arthur. 106-113: Frederic F. Bigio from B-C Graphics. 114: Fil Hunter. 116-119: John Massey. 121-123: Frederic F. Bigio from B-C Graphics. 125, 126: Elsie J. Hennig. 129-133: Walter Hilmers Jr. from H-J Commercial Art.

Acknowledgments

The index/glossary for this book was prepared by Louis Hedberg. The editors also wish to thank the following: Ivan Bailey, Bailey's Forge, Savannah, Ga.; Steve Bondi, San Anselmo, Calif.; The Buffalo Forge Company, Buffalo, N.Y.; Dr. Hallock Campbell, American Welding Society, Miami, Fla.; Copper Development Association, New York, N.Y.; Doug Cornell, Aluminum Association, Washington, D.C.; Dwyer Service Corporation, Alexandria, Va.; Margot Gayle, New York, N.Y.; Dr. Lee Grant, Agricultural Engineering Department, University of Maryland, College Park, Md.; Dr. Michael A. Greenfield, Program Manager for Materials, Office of Aeronautics and Space Technology, National Aeronautics and Space Administration, Washington, D.C.; John T. Heine, Bosco Welding Supply, Alexandria, Va.; Johnson Gas Appliance Company, Cedar Rapids, Iowa; Philip J. Joyce Sr., Hopewell, Pa.; The Lincoln Electric Company, Cleveland, Ohio; Diane Maddox, Preservation Press, National Trust for Historic Preservation, Washington, D.C.; Metal Distributing Company, Inc., Alexandria, Va.; Milwaukee Tool and Equipment Company, Milwaukee, Wis.; Richard Ruskay, New York, N.Y.; Virginia Roofing Corporation, Alexandria, Va.; Welding Engineering and Equipment Company, Beltsville, Md. The editors would also like to express their appreciation to George Bond, William Doyle, Edgar Henry, Mark Schaffer, David Shapiro, Wendy Shay and Steve Smith, writers, for their assistance with the preparation of this volume.

Index/Glossary